GETTING YOUR CHILDREN THROUGH DIVORCE

GETTING YOUR CHILDREN THROUGH DIVORCE

A parent's guide to separation

ANNE HOOPER

ROBSON BOOKS

First published in Great Britain in 2005 by Robson Books, The Chrysalis Building, Bramley Road, London W10 6SP

An imprint of **Chrysalis** Books Group plc

The author has made every reasonable effort to contact all copyright holders. Any errors that may have occurred are inadvertent and anyone who for any reason has not been contacted is invited to write to the publishers so that a full acknowledgement may be made in subsequent editions of this work.

British Library Cataloguing in Publication Data
A catalogue record for this title is available from the British Library.

ISBN 1 86105 915 9

Printed by Creative Print and Design Wales, Ebbw Vale

CONTENTS

To my extended family
To Phillip, Brian, Barnaby, Joel and Alexander

PREFACE

When I and my ex-husband separated many years ago, there was not one single book that helped parents explain divorce to children or that offered advice on how the children might react. Fired with angry need, I set to on producing such a book. It was the first of its kind in the United Kingdom. Over the years it has been published in three separate and different editions, recommended by family court judges to divorcing couples and heavily borrowed via the library system.

Thirty years on

I optimistically hoped that, thirty years later, conciliation and mediation services would have developed so fully that a book like mine would no longer be needed. Alas! it seems to be needed more than ever. Fifty per cent of dads still lose touch with their families after divorce even though a vociferous minority (as represented by Families Need Fathers, a well-publicised pressure group in the UK) continue to fight for their 'rights' as parents. Fifty per cent of mums struggle to bring up their children with little or no support. All of this impacts on the children, who of course are the innocent parties in separation and divorce.

Help is needed!

How little help there still is for separating parents was brought home to me recently when a young friend and colleague needed assistance. She wanted to explain to her four-year-old why Daddy had moved out. On searching the bookshops she couldn't find a single book focused primarily on these sensitive conversations. The bookshelves hold several reports on the long-term effects of divorce on children (it's not as damaging as you might expect), but a slim volume that concentrates on sitting down with the children and talking was surprisingly absent.

That is why I am radically rewriting and updating my original book *Divorce and Your Children* in order to bring it back into print. We republish it here under the title *Getting Your Children through Divorce*. Taking my younger colleague's need seriously, I have focused in this edition almost entirely on the children's emotional welfare. Where I write about relations between husband and wife, it is always done from the first principle of 'what will be best for the children'!

Fight to control your anger and fear

Critics will probably say when they leaf through these pages that I'm wearing rose-coloured spectacles. The whole problem with separation, they will insist, is that you feel so gutted by painful emotion it's impossible to deal in a civilised manner with the person who is hurting you, even in order to help the children. My reply is that such self-control is of course extremely difficult, but I have to say, *not* impossible. Increasing numbers of parents manage it these days – if not on their own, then with the help of mediation counsellors. And when you understand how much your 'civilised' behaviour matters to your children, I really hope you will at least consider the advice offered here with an open mind.

LATEST RESEARCH

Just before we move swiftly to the nitty-gritty of childcare, you may care to get a grip on a few useful new facts to emerge from the most up-to-date research on divorce and children.

In 2002 a huge study of 2,500 children of divorce who were observed for thirty years by Professor Mavis Hetherington of the University of Virginia revealed that:

- The great majority (between 75 and 80 per cent) showed very little *long-term* damage and, as adults, were functioning well.
- Specifically, *within two years* of the parents' separation the great majority were doing well.
- These figures also mean of course that 25 per cent of children did *not* do so well.

So just why is adjustment to divorce easier for some children than others? Another huge survey carried out by the Joseph Rowntree Foundation (2004) suggested that:

- Family conflict both *before and after* separation makes life much harder for the children.
- Parental ability to recover from the distress of separation affects the children's ability to adjust.
- Multiple changes in family structure increase the probability of distress later.
- Quality contact with the non-resident parent can improve the children's emotional well-being.

However, the study also found that, contrary to popular belief:

- The absence of a parent figure is *not* the most influential feature of separation for the children's development.

WHAT'S IN THE BOOK

The main bulk of the book focuses on how to break the news of divorce or separation, and later on how to get your children through the first difficult months. I also include a completely new chapter on specific parenting techniques that can be used by any parent, be they separated or together. These techniques:

- offer methods of helping the children talk about their feelings
- assist them to take on reasonable responsibilities
- encourage them in their achievements
- offer the children a sense of being in control of their life (very important when so much feels out of their control)
- give the children a sense of self-worth and self-value.

Present-day divorce statistics

According to the government's Green Paper *Every Child Matters*, published in 2003, around 150,000 couples divorce per year in the UK. Around two-thirds of the families concerned include children under the age of sixteen. In addition there is an unknown but substantial number of men and women who separate after living together and who also have children under the age of sixteen. At least one in three children will experience parental separation before the age of sixteen.

①

SEPARATION – STEP BY STEP

However much we may feel like taking a meat axe to our former partner, most of us understand that, if we are parents, we need to curb our murderous instincts and focus on our children instead. Children are the innocent parties in all the mess and confusion. Most of us, who care deeply about our offspring, want to manage this distressing situation in the best possible way as far as they are concerned.

The most common questions asked by separating parents are:

- What do we tell the children?
- How do we tell the children?
- What are the best ways to support them?
- How long do we continue in such emergency parenting mode?

So here, without any further waffle about the pain of marital in-fighting, are the step-by-step moves that you and your partner can make, either singly or together, to explain your new decision to the children and to subsequently help them through their various feelings.

MOVE ONE. TAKE TIME OVER YOUR SEPARATION

This may not sound directly relevant to your children's needs, but it is. To deal well with your children it helps to take just that little bit of extra time, painful though it may be, to jointly decide on how best to prepare and provide for them. Even if it takes as much as one month or three to make the actual break, that's all right.

There is no rule to say one partner is forced to move away from home the minute a couple decide to separate. Just because the partner doesn't leave immediately, it doesn't mean the departure will never happen. It indicates rather that these are mature people taking a great deal of care over one of the most important decisions of a lifetime.

Don't let anyone tell you anything different and don't let any friend, relation or (particularly) lover hustle you away from your family until you feel sure you have made reasonable preparation for your departure.

Of course, not all of us possess the luxury of extra time. Feelings may simply be too violent or actions taken too quickly to plan the family's future together. The next move therefore is to be supportive to the children.

MOVE TWO. PLAN YOUR CHILDREN'S FUTURE

In order to give the children a clear picture of what is going to happen to them, the two parents should have worked out the following by the time you break the news. You need to decide:

- which parent will move out
- where that parent will live

- what accommodation will be there for the children. Will they have their own rooms? Will they share a room? Will they get a special area in a room that is specifically theirs?
- how much detail you disclose about your reasons for separating. The children will need a proper explanation, even though it's worded simply.

Children need to know what to expect.

MOVE THREE. REASSURE YOUR CHILDREN

The children will realise something disturbing is going on even if they don't know what it is. If they are very young, they may show their unease by becoming difficult and tearful. When you too are feeling difficult and tearful it is hard to cope with an extra emotional burden, but try to remember that you are *all* suffering, so be extra nice to them. Your tasks:

- Give extra cuddles.
- Make time for explanations.

MOVE FOUR. TRY TO ANTICIPATE THE CHILDREN'S EMOTIONAL REACTIONS

The important question is, 'What will your children need the *most* reassurance about?' If you can gain some insight into that, it helps you prepare the answers that may be needed. Of course, particularly with young children, it's hard to predict. But you can attempt an informed guess.

Golden rules

- It is important to tell the children the news yourselves and to do so before anyone else (e.g. a relative or neighbour) says the wrong thing at the wrong time in front of them.
- It is also vital to be honest, and *not* to hide any of the relevant facts – for example, that one parent has already left home. When parents avoid talking about their separation, the children's fears are magnified and they replace reality with fantasy and imaginary defences. Over-protection can hurt them. It is often easier for them to face a painful reality than an anguished uncertainty.
- It is also desirable for both parents to tell the children *together*, however hard this may be. If both parents are there, it is easier *to avoid putting all the blame on to one or the other*. And it is better for the children, because it means they do not have to take sides.

The more conflict that emerges in telling the children, the more insecure they will feel. These disclosures therefore should be held, if possible, during an emotional lull in the separation. If held immediately after a bitter argument, the details will emerge in an angry way and will hurt and confuse the children.

The most important reassurance of all

This needs to be stressed over and over again – you *both* love the children. *Just because you no longer love each other, this does not mean that you don't love them.* You do. It is a *vital* message, which must be got across.

MOVE FIVE. ANSWER YOUR CHILDREN'S IMMEDIATE QUESTIONS

What each child wants to know will vary from one individual to another. Most generally, though, their questions will focus on:

- *learning what will happen*, how soon it will happen and where
- *hearing an explanation*, however brief, about why the divorce is happening. This is important because children commonly blame themselves for the break-up.
- *getting reassurance* that each parent separately and individually wants and has every intention of remaining closely involved with the children. This might take the form of explaining what the childcare arrangements will be. And the access arrangements should start *as soon as the departing parent has left*.

Your baby

Of course a baby can't ask questions and won't understand what is happening. However, a baby can pick up tensions like anyone else and although there is no way you will be able to avoid your feelings of pain and hurt (indeed you need these as a normal part of grieving), you can be ready to give that baby extra cuddles, extra attention and to understand if he/she seems to fret and cry more than usual.

Your toddler

As soon as your child begins to acquire some language, he/she also acquires some understanding. Be prepared for simple questions that deserve simple answers. (See 'How to Break the News', page 6.) Make with the cuddles!

Your young children

If the children are through the toddler stage they are going to want rather more detail. They will need to know what will happen to them. Typical questions they may ask are:

- Who will they live with?
- Will their toys go with them?
- Are they going to move house? District? Even country?
- Will school be changed?
- Who will look after them?
- Will they still have the same old friends?

Your task is to be prepared with simple answers.

Your older children

They may want to know more about the social implications of your separation.

- Are the relatives going to think badly of them?
- Will they become curiosities at school?
- Whose fault is it?

Again your job is to be prepared with answers offered at a level of simplicity that they will be able to understand. For more details, see below.

HOW TO BREAK THE NEWS

Starting the explanation

A good way to disclose something distressing is to hold your children close (especially if they are young) while you talk. Your body warmth will do a lot to reassure them and show them that they are not being abandoned. In fact this closeness will help a child of any age.

Explain that you and Daddy/Mummy are not happy living together and therefore you are going to live apart; that you will both cheer up and become happier people when this happens, even if it takes a while. If you have been having a lot of distressing rows, you could say, 'I expect you've noticed we haven't been very happy lately.'

It is not necessary to go into detail about the rows. Too much detail can be confusing for young children, although older children may *want* to know. Many children may already be upset and confused from overhearing the fights. If they ask specific questions, they should be given specific answers, but certainly *not* a list of every single accusation or a blow-by-blow account of your quarrels.

For example. Rather than describe how Daddy has victimised Mummy over spending money on her clothes or how Mummy has run Daddy into the ground with her avaricious demands, it is quite enough to say simply that you have found it impossible to agree over money and your disagreements are now so strong that it has become impossible to live happily together any more.

To the parents, immersed in one of the most traumatic upheavals of their lives, these disputes seem of paramount importance. And so they are, but *only to them*. The quarrels which loom so large in *their* lives are irrelevant to their children. All the children want is for the fighting to stop.

Separation anxieties

Children, especially young children, suffer from separation anxieties. A secure child is one who knows that everything in the home is in its place. When one parent moves out, therefore, the children's world shifts. It is genuinely shocking. This is why a parent should *never* move out overnight with no warning. The impact can be devastating. Instead the parents should jointly explain what is going to happen, should offer a date for when it is scheduled and should immediately explain that of course the departing parent has arranged a room (or at the least a specific area, e.g. a corner of the room) for the children to stay in. This way the children understand that there is a very definite place for them in the departing parent's life.

A supportive atmosphere

Once you have made the actual announcement, you can expect a variety of questions to be asked, to which you will need to give simple but truthful answers. One of the most supportive ways to hold this conversation is in a group. (In Chapter 12 I describe how to hold a family meeting.) Children get support from such a group. It may be helpful to have other loving relations present. Possible candidates might be grandparents, cousins, aunts and uncles, godparents or even a close family friend, all of whom will have had some briefing before the meeting. When everyone is included, the children immediately feel that there is support around them.

SUMMARY

- Work out your explanation beforehand, preferably together.
- Tell your children together, if preferred in a family group.
- Keep it simple.

②
WHAT TO TELL THE CHILDREN

It is impossible to anticipate *all* those innocently provocative questions. 'Mummy, why doesn't Daddy like you any more?' was the one that floored me personally. But you can certainly prepare yourself for a few. The questions that follow here may be asked when you give your very first explanations. However, in my experience, children go away and quietly mull over the issues. These questions then pop out *later* at unexpected intervals. They still need to be answered though!

The following is a list of the most common questions. The answers have been gleaned from friends, child psychologists, social workers and personal experience. Of course, when you come to reply to your children you will use your own words. My suggestions here are just hints as to how to go about it. The essence of these explanations lies in expressing yourself straightforwardly, in reassuring the children, and in not overdoing the bitter feelings you may well possess towards your spouse or partner.

The questions and answers have been worded for families where it is Dad who has left home. They will, of course, be very similar when it is Mum who has moved out. The explanations have been geared for a young child. Naturally, you will need to interpret them at a level to suit your own offspring.

Q Why are you getting divorced?

A Because we haven't been getting along very well together. We've been unhappy for a long time. So now we think we might be happier if we live in separate homes.

Q Why did Daddy go away?

A (*The answer may either be much as above or, if he has gone to live with another woman . . .*) Because Daddy and Mummy haven't been very happy living together for quite a long time and now Daddy has met another woman with whom he thinks he *will* be happier. But Daddy still loves *you* very much and you will see him every week.

(*There's no point in beating around the bush. But it is important to reassure the children that Daddy still loves them, even if he doesn't love their mother any more.*)

Q If you love Daddy so much, why did he leave?

A You can still love someone but find him very hard to live with. Both Daddy and I have been finding each other hard to live with. So we have decided to find different homes. But there will always be a home for you with me and you will have fun visiting Daddy often in his new flat.

(*This is a tricky question because it is a loaded one. It is important not to let the children make a connection with Daddy leaving Mummy even though she still loves him, and Daddy leaving the children, who also love him. It must be emphasised that, although the mother has been rejected, the children have not.*)

Q But how can someone stop loving you?

A It's like forgetting someone very slowly. If you don't think about them very much, slowly you forget to love that person. Perhaps your love goes to a new person instead and that takes up the space of the old love. But Daddy is *not* going to forget or stop loving you. That's why he wants to see you at the weekends and in the holidays.

Q Will you still both be my mummy and daddy?
A We will always be your mummy and daddy. Nothing can ever, ever change that.

Q Will my brothers and sisters be with me?
A (*Obviously depends on child custody arrangements.*) *Either:* Yes, we will all carry on living together except for Daddy. *Or:* Your older brother (Brian) is going to live with Daddy and you are going to stay here with me. But we will all meet up often. And sometimes you will stay with Daddy and Brian and sometimes Brian will stay with you and me.

Q Why can't *I* go and live with Daddy?
A Because till you are older we think you will have a better time living with me. And, besides, I need you to keep me company. And Daddy needs Brian to keep him company.

Q I don't want you as my mummy any more. Why can't I live with my daddy?
(*This child is directing her anger about the divorce at the nearest available parent. Don't rise to the bait. And don't waver in your confidence about the custody arrangements. The more she senses your feelings that the arrangements made are the right ones, the more she is going to feel secure. The angry child is also the one who is most likely to need a very big cuddle of reassurance at night.*)
A I can understand that you feel angry about Daddy and me living apart. That's perfectly natural. And of course it won't be the

same without Daddy. But it will be fun in a different way and we will be able to do different things. One of the things I thought we might do that was different would be to buy a dog. How do you feel about that?

(*For children over five years old, a dog is a sensible new project as it is something for them to direct their confused emotions towards, something to take their minds off their parents' problems, and a manifestation of the good part of your new life. It should not be offered in any way which makes it seem like a bribe or to replace a parent, but simply as one of the several new schemes that this altered family unit is exploring.*)

Q I don't want to live with you, Mummy. I want to go and live with my dad.

(*One of the main things resented by any child is the feeling of helplessness often experienced through being a child and therefore having no real control over life. The absent parent often seems more glamorous and attractive than the mundane old parent the child lives with. This combination of feelings makes children particularly sensitive to being thwarted and therefore they need to assert their independence. The more you can alleviate the feeling of helplessness, the better they will feel about their self-value. If they know that, they will feel less helpless and trapped.*)

A You will be able to spend loads of time with Dad. You can get on the phone any time you want to speak to him. And as soon as you are old enough, you can ride your bicycle round to his place whenever you feel like it.

(*Some children are given their own mobiles by their parents – who top them up rather than have a bill sent to them – so they can keep in touch. Many older children these days can also use email. French and American studies of divorced children have* shown that the children with the most flexible access arrangements tend to be able to adjust best to divorce. Being able to ride a bike round to the other parent's house is specifically advocated in an American survey.)

Q I still want to go and live with my dad. Why can't I?
(*There comes a stage where the children will have to get used to the idea that, while everything possible will be arranged to keep them happy, they have got to accept that the decision for them to remain with their mother has been made by people more experienced than they are – who, should you need to get down to the nitty-gritty, know better than they do. If they do not like it, gently but firmly make it clear that their feelings are unfortunate but that they will have to put up with and make the best of the present arrangements.*)

A We have both decided it is better for you to remain with *me*, though you can see Daddy often.
(*Be prepared to say this politely but firmly several times over the next few weeks – until they get used to it. It is important for the parent with custody to keep an open mind about access arrangements, however. If over a period of, say, a year, the child remains unhappy and becomes increasingly depressed, you may well have made the wrong decision and it would therefore be wise to change it. But it won't help things to be wishy-washy about the decision at the start of the separation.*)

Q Why do you keep asking if I'm OK? I don't want to talk about you and Daddy any more.
(*Some children find it very difficult to discuss their feelings with a parent, simply because the conversation will be highly charged emotionally, especially if the children have seen many arguments and fights between the mother and father. It does*

not mean that there isn't a turmoil going on underneath their silence. If you have good reason to believe a child is very upset but is bottling it up, this is one of the occasions where it might be sensible to take her to a children's counsellor. It could be that she will find it easier to talk to a stranger than to talk to her emotive parents.)

A I'm sorry, darling, I don't want to upset you. But I care about you and if you're feeling bad, I'd like to help you to feel better. Perhaps you would feel more comfortable talking to a children's doctor without either of us there to listen.

(If the answer is 'No', she doesn't want to talk to anyone at all, don't push it. She is entitled to the privacy of her thoughts, and may simply be trying to avoid something that causes her pain. One way of getting her to unburden herself a little is to talk about her other friends. If any of their parents are divorced, ask how the friend feels. This gives her the opportunity to drop a few clues about her own feelings.)

Q Mummy, why doesn't Daddy like you any more?

A Because he's feeling very angry with me at the moment for wanting to divorce. I hope he'll like me better later on when he's got used to the idea.

Q Daddy says you've done something bad to him. What is it?

A I think he means that the bad thing was wanting to divorce. He feels badly about that right now.

Q Mummy, you say you love Daddy even though you want to divorce. Does that mean that it's Daddy's fault you are divorcing?

A No, it's never just one person's fault. And you can love someone as well as dislike them. Look at you. Sometimes you love me, sometimes you hate me when you get mad at me. Daddy and I were finding it hard to live together happily so we decided to change things. But there will always be a home for you with either of us. *So you've always got both your parents to rely on, even if they are living in two different places.*

Q Which one of you will look after me?

A It will be mostly me. I shall do most of the things I always have done – the cooking, getting your clothes ready, taking you to school. And on the days when you're with Daddy, *he* will cook for you and look after you. (*If Daddy hasn't done much in the way of housework previously, reassure her that he knows how.*) Daddy *can* cook, you know, he used to prepare terrific meals before we married.

Q What shall I tell my friends?

A Just tell them that your parents are getting divorced and that you will be living with your mummy. If they want to know more, they'll ask you.

Q Mummy, you won't ever love anyone again like you did Daddy, will you?

A I won't ever love anyone in the same way as Daddy because you can only love Daddy like Daddy. But I might love someone else very much too.

(*Don't let yourself be emotionally blackmailed into saying things you don't mean and might regret later.*)

Q Mummy, when are you going to get married to Daddy again?

(*This may be confused thinking on the part of the children, but it is more likely to be wishful thinking. Simply explain gently but firmly for the hundredth time that you and Daddy are no longer living together, that you will not be getting married again to each other, that from now on you and he are leading separate lives. It can be hard to be firm about this when you have wistful youngsters badly wanting you to get back together again. But you will only be doing them a disservice if you give them false hopes with vague hints of a reunion. It is better that they face the truth.)*

A Sorry darling. I know this feels hard but your Daddy and I will not be getting back together again.

Q Mummy, why does Granny say that Daddy is no good?

A *(Make mental note to get very heavy with Granny.)* She doesn't really mean that Daddy's no good. What she means is that she's angry with him because of the divorce. She thinks it's all his fault. It isn't. But when Granny gets an idea into her head, it's sometimes very hard to change it. By calling him no good, she's really telling us that she's very cross.

Q Mummy, why don't you like Daddy any more?

A *(Be truthful about your reasons while resisting the temptation to reel off a long list of Daddy's faults.)* I need someone who is going to be able to help me more with my family and will do his share of the work in the house. Your daddy has lots of other nice things going for him, but not those. And those things happen to be important to me.

Q Why were you so nasty to Daddy? If you'd been nicer he would have stayed with us.

A I was nasty because I was unhappy with Daddy. And when a person is unhappy they often behave badly. I wasn't the only one who was nasty, you know. Daddy was pretty unpleasant too.

(*This child has obviously worked out from the rows she has overheard that it is Mummy who has driven her father away. This may be true but she still needs some sort of an explanation.*)

Q Are you going to get married again?

A (*Obviously depends on what your plans are. If you have no immediate plans, leave doors open:*) Not at the moment, darling, but I probably will one day. I might marry my friend Michael one day. But I'm not really sure at the moment. I certainly hope I *will* get married again one day.

(*Resist the temptation to swear never again. Because if you do go ahead and remarry later on, your children may remember this and find it harder to adapt to a new husband. On the other hand, if you are contemplating remarriage, and soon, but haven't yet told your children, introduce the possibility gradually. It's too much to expect them to adapt to an instant change in daddies.*)

Q Did Daddy leave because of Michael?

A Daddy and I had been getting along badly for a long time. Michael happened to come along at a particularly bad time and made me realise I would be much happier with him.

(*Even if Daddy* did *leave because of Michael, it's better not to pin the responsibility on the possible new stepfather's shoulders at this emotional stage of the separation.*)

Q It's all my fault that Daddy went away, isn't it?

A No, it's not. It has absolutely nothing to do with you, or with anything you've done. The reason Daddy has gone away is because he was unhappy with me, not with you. He loves you very much indeed and will be seeing you as much as he possibly can.

(It is vital to dispel any fears or notions children may have that something they have done is responsible for the marriage break-up. It is very common for a child to think this, and unless the idea is removed, it can result in some very depressed and unhappy behaviour.)

Q Now that Daddy's gone, does that mean I'm an orphan?

A Definitely not. An orphan is a child whose parents have both died. Your parents are very much alive and kicking and concerned about your welfare.

Q Mummy, was it your fault that Daddy found a new girlfriend?

A It was nobody's fault. Daddy had stopped loving me and obviously needed some other lady to love, so he found his new friend.

Q Mummy, when will you find a new daddy for me?

A It's not so easy to find good new husbands. They are rather special people. But I'm keeping an eye open.

(It is often important to children that everything in their life conforms. It is quite possible that you will find yourself pressurised by your child to make everything regular at home, by providing her with a permanent living-in dad, even though he is not the original one. This might be the time to make a mental note to ensure that she gets more male company, either in the form of more access to her father, or with her uncles, or simply with old friends who happen to be male. It sounds as if she is needing it. But don't let yourself get pushed into marrying someone simply because he seems a suitable stepfather. He also needs to be a suitable husband.)

Q When is Michael going to leave? I don't like him.

(*Child asks about Mummy's boyfriend who is now living with them and who shortly intends to marry Mummy.*)

A I'm sorry you don't like him. I expect you are jealous of his being Mummy's friend. But I'm afraid you will have to get used to living with Michael because he's going to be around for a long time. He loves me which is very nice for me. *You* have two people to love you, a mummy and a daddy. Well, I would like two people to love me as well, you and Michael.

(*It's not a good idea to thrust the possibility of your remarriage down your children's throats before they have had time to get used to your new partner. At the same time, they must gently but firmly be made to understand that you like him even though they don't. I believe in letting your children know when somebody loves you, even if they are jealous and resentful, because someone else's love and affection enhances a personal value about you that may well have been thrown out of the window by your previous partner during the marriage break-up. It is important that the children should have their feelings that you are a valuable person reinforced, even if the process does bring conflicting jealousies. It is easy for a child to feel emotionally responsible for the parent 'left behind', and this can be a heavy burden for a young person. You are effectively letting them off that hook if they can see that you are self-confident in yourself and valued by someone else.*)

Q Are you going to marry Michael?

A I may do, darling. I'm not quite sure at the moment. But I'm certainly enjoying dating him/living with him. If things keep on as well as they have done so far, it would be very nice to marry. But I'm not in any hurry.

(*I repeat, this is* not *the time to say 'Yes'. Your children need time to get used to this confusing change of male figures in their lives.*)

Q Will Daddy die now that he's away from us?

A No, of course not, darling. He'll carry on working at his job and doing the same sort of things in his new home that he used to do here. He will be all right. He can take care of himself, you know. He's a big, grown-up man. He certainly won't die.

Q Why won't you buy me new toys any more?

A Because now that Daddy isn't living with us we don't have nearly so much money. What we do have has to be spent on important things like food and keeping warm, and on paying for our home. I wish we had a little extra to spend on playthings but unfortunately we don't. But we'll try and make some toys so that you've got something new to play with.

(*Make a mental note to enrol the child at the local library (free) if she is old enough to enjoy books and to investigate, through the library, the possibility of locating a toy library or using the library computers.*)

Q Did Daddy leave because I didn't love him enough?

(*Another typical example of how children think it is their fault that Daddy left home. They have probably associated his departure with the last time they got the sulks and behaved badly, or with some small slight on their part.*)

A Daddy's leaving has nothing to do with you at all. He didn't go because of anything you said or did or even thought. He left because he and *I* could not agree. Daddy loves you very, very much.

Q How should I explain your divorce to my friends?

A The best thing is to tell them what we have told you. Explain that your mummy and daddy are getting a divorce because they found it difficult to live together happily any more, therefore they have decided to live in two separate homes. So, from now on, you are going to have two homes. You'll probably find that some of your friends' parents are divorced as well.

Q Should I do the same with my relations?

A Yes, but be prepared for some of them to be very surprised at the news. Some people may be upset about it. I'm warning you about them so that *they* don't surprise and upset *you*.

Q Mummy, do you hate Daddy's new girlfriend?

A I don't like her very much because I'm angry with her for taking Daddy away. But I don't hate her. I expect I'll get used to her eventually, even though that's hard to imagine right now.
(*This tells the truth, yet shows that adults are capable of changing their feelings in the same way that children are.*)

It is important to understand that children go through a long period of trying to work out these major changes in their lives, why they happened and what these circumstances have to do with *them*. It is as natural for the children to need to talk about *their* feelings (in order to sort them out) as it is for you.

If any of you are bottling up terrible sad feelings, both parents and children should try to understand it is a good idea to get them out *somehow*. Even if it's hard for *you*, the bereft parent, to find someone to talk things over with, at least you should have the satisfaction of knowing you can provide a platform for discussion for your children.

SUMMARY

- Answer questions truthfully but simply.
- Be prepared to answer the same question many times over the following weeks.
- Resist the temptation to bad-mouth your ex-partner.
- If at all possible, try to work with your ex-partner to ensure that you give a reasonably similar account of events. Of course this is not always possible!

③

YOUR CHILDREN'S REACTIONS

Your children will react to the news of your separation in several ways. Obviously their understanding of what this means will be shaped by their age and stage of development. There are several commonly experienced signs of grief (which I explain below). It's unlikely the children will have a handle on the bigger picture. But they are highly likely to wonder what will happen to them. They are going to want clear reassurances that as much as possible of their present lifestyle will survive the change. Your challenge here is to offer reassurance while explaining that there have to be some differences. And expect to be asked the same questions over and over again.

IMMEDIATE REACTIONS

Questioning

This may not happen when you first break the news but it is highly likely to recur over the ensuing weeks. It is very hard for anyone to take in the fact that two people are divorcing or separating. The world shifts and rocks at such announcements. The children's need for repeated explanations is their method of coping with and working through the perplexing situation. Be prepared to give details time and again.

Crying

If your children cry, don't try to make them stop or tell them to 'be brave'. Crying is good for them – it is a natural expression of their grief. If you teach them to bottle up their feelings and repress their grief, they may find this grief crops up in later life on a range of inappropriate occasions.

My own five-year-old burst into tears instantly and then stopped almost as quickly. He moved off to play with his cousin and didn't say much more that day. But the questions arrived at regular intervals for at least six months afterwards. His younger brother, then aged three, showed no visible reaction. I've often wondered if he understood just what we were talking about.

Little overt reaction

If the children appear to have little or no reaction to your news, don't be too surprised. It may mean they have not yet had time to feel the impact of what they have just been told. This will become more apparent via the questions they ask during the following weeks.

It's their fault

One common misguided belief is that the children think *they* have somehow managed to cause the divorce. Their experiences may have taught them that when they are good they are rewarded, and when they are bad they are punished. Divorce can therefore seem like retribution. The children may search their minds for something 'wicked' they have done, which they feel has caused the split.

For example, one girl remembered a time in the past when she and her brother had been particularly noisy. Their father, in a fit of annoyance, had yelled at her that he couldn't stand it when she fought with her brother. She was later convinced it was because she had carried on fighting after being asked not to that her father had been driven away from home.

Often these feelings of childish guilt may seem inexplicable and unlikely to parents, who are inclined to dismiss them. But they are real enough to the children, which is why each parent should repeat to their offspring over and over again that they are unhappy with each other, *not* with the children.

THE SIGNS OF GRIEF

Although grief affects children individually (depending on age and experience), it usually contains several well-recognised stages. These are not always experienced in the order listed below but classically they consist of:

Shock

This may result in a child instantly bursting into tears and just as instantly getting over the tears and wanting to go back to play; exploding into a frenzy of screaming; looking dazed and uncom-prehending or almost visibly withdrawing; not wanting to talk, cry or let go of any emotion. The younger the child, the more confusing the news of a divorce is likely to be, since they don't really understand what is happening but can pick up easily enough the general impression that something very unpleasant is going on at home.

How you can help. Comfort, cuddling, hugging and holding is vitally important, but distraction from the emotional reaction is a poor idea. It merely bottles up strong feelings and makes it harder for these to emerge later. Talk to children about the meaning of your separation, as calmly and lovingly as you can manage.

Anger

Your announcements may bring an angry reaction either immediately or, just as likely, later, after the children have had time to think about the news. This may come via actions rather than words, lying down and kicking, attacking toys or a baby brother or sister.

How you can help. It's important to acknowledge the feelings behind the actions directly, while at the same time trying to provide the children with some other method of working off their anger. Get them to dance very energetically. Give them a 'hit' cushion especially for punching or utilise any of your tried and true family methods for expelling rage.

Sadness

As the children think over the changes during the days following your announcement, this may bring on waves of sadness as they realise that nothing will ever be quite the same again. Crying, weeping, sometimes for unexpected reasons such as the realisation that Dad (or Mum) will no longer be there in the evening to turn to with homework, are typical.

How you can help. Don't stop the children from weeping – they need to get their sadness out. Agree with them that this is very hard. But after you have had a cry, tell them something more cheerful about the future, such as the fact that Dad is going to take them away on holiday soon. This way they get to grieve but they also acquire hope.

Denial

It is sometimes *so* threatening to think of your family as never being the same again that some children just can't accept it. Even though they understand what has been explained, they will tell themselves and their friends that Dad has gone away for a while but is expected back any day now. This of course embodies wishful thinking and is the cause of repeated questioning to the parent left behind, along the lines of 'Mum, when is Dad coming back?'

How you can help. Don't insist that their father has gone but use natural openings in the conversation to explain yet again that Daddy is now living on the other side of town. Assertiveness training describes something called the 'dripping tap technique'. This consists of simply stating the same facts over and over until they eventually impact on the brain, much as constant water impacts on a stone.

Searching

Alongside such wishful thinking goes a pattern of constantly looking for the departed parent everywhere. 'Will he be coming back tonight?' 'Is that her car in the road?' 'Could that be my daddy picking me up from school?'

How you can help. The best way to deal with denial and searching is not to argue with it or get impatient but to tell the children that these are very common behaviours shown by many people when feeling sad and experiencing a loss. If you find that you too are behaving in a similar way, you could share your feelings with the children, so that you are brought closer together in your mourning.

Anxiety

It is also common when experiencing such loss that children fear other things will be lost too, such as their best toy or their best friend. Hence there is a real need for keeping as much as possible of the children's life as intact as it was before the separation.

How you can help. Of course, this isn't always feasible, but if you can manage to arrange at least one or two constants – such as (1) your continued presence and (2) the children's attendance at the same school – this is a great help.

Guilt

'Was it all my fault that Dad went away?' 'Was it something I did?' and 'Unless I behave in a certain way, always folding my clothes as Dad liked me to, perhaps something else will go wrong too.' These are classic reactions to divorce and need constant reassurance from each parent.

How you can help. Emphasise regularly, using natural openings in your conversations, that *nothing* the children did or said was responsible for what happened between you and their dad.

Depression

Many of the things that worsen depression are worries about practical problems such as 'How will I get to school in the morning, now that Dad's taken the car with him?' 'Will I still get pocket money if we're going to be poorer?' If your children felt terribly sad before, these worries could be enough to make them quiet, fearful and depressed.

How you can help. Recognising that their worries have meaning and offering practical backup and support is vital to help the children feel better. Comfort and a listening ear are needed. Reduced financial circumstances are one of the factors known to particularly upset and worry children of separated parents. See if a grandparent can give pocket money. Arrange for a school pick-up system with another parent. When the child is older, help him realise that he can begin to earn too. Saturday jobs and paper rounds are the best way to start.

Despair

Sometimes even the parent with the very best of intentions cannot pick up the significant clues or cues and a child falls into a deep depression.

How you can help. This is when outside professional help needs to be called in. Family counsellors, educational psychologists and counsellors specialising in child and teenage difficulties are among those able to provide really practical assistance.

HOW DOES YOUR GRIEF IMPACT ON YOUR CHILDREN?

Grief is real. If you deny grief you deny reality. And if you possess sad feelings it is healthy to let them out. There is nothing weak or indulgent about this. In order to help our children, therefore, we often have to *acknowledge needs and pain of our own*. So if in the early days of separation you, the parent, feel like crying (because everywhere you turn there is some reminder of the person and life you are losing), let yourself cry.

It's OK to cry alongside the children

Don't cut the children off from your crying. If you do so you place them in an artificial situation. They will know your feelings anyway. Children sense all kinds of unspoken emotion and will probably want to cry alongside you. It's fine and healthy for a family to express grief together. *It feels like a safe context in which to sorrow.* So don't be closed in with your own mourning. It's OK to cry with your kids, at least to begin with.

What you are doing by talking about your feelings and crying is acknowledging that separation and divorce are major life changes, in some ways worse to bear than death. Death is at least aided by the ritual of funeral where there is a public acknowledgement of your sorrow. Divorce doesn't have such a rite of passage, which makes it somehow more complicated to endure.

How much grief is too much?

Listen to your child. Even very small children can be staggeringly direct with their view of the situation. Four-year-old Amelia was overheard telling her little friend not to cry any more. 'My Mummy cries all the time,' she told her friend. 'I want you to have some fun.' Translated, this could well mean Amelia would also like some fun for a change.

The trouble with crying too much is that *you leave no room to attend to the feelings of others*. Of course it's understandable if you cry every now and again, over the next few months, at poignant reminders. But you need to do this quietly and in private. It's important to remember that one of the factors that over-stress children of divorce and separation and give them a poor outcome in the future is for a parent to show *constant* deep distress. If you care about your children you need to sort out long-term feelings of grief.

HOW TO HELP YOUR CHILDREN GRIEVE

Your children's grief won't be the same as yours!

Even while you experience your own sadness, it is sensible to try and understand the level of your children's grief. *For it won't be the same as yours.*

- Children with a father they hardly ever see because of the demands of his work may sense very little loss.
- Children with a father with whom they constantly fight may feel relief at not having to fight any more, but also guilt at that relief.

- Children who have been close to their father will miss him as a companion. If it is the mother who has left (and one in eight do), similar rules apply.
- A career woman who has left her children to the care of a nanny during the marriage may either be unconsidered by her children at separation or, more likely, deeply regretted because now they may never have the opportunity to get close to her. Each case is unique.

What can you do?

Create deliberate areas of calm for the children in which to find out how *they* are feeling. This means creating deliberate areas of calm for yourself. Cry at other times if need be, but *cry elsewhere*. Wait till the children go out before howling. Bottle yourself up until they've gone to school. Get your mother or a friend to take them off your hands at regular intervals. Be practical about giving yourself grieving time.

Use calm times

During those quieter periods, give the children opportunities to talk about *their* thoughts and sorrows. Simple questions such as 'How are you feeling today?' 'How has your day been?' 'What was school like today?' can be productive. More specifically, 'I wonder what Daddy is doing now?' or 'Did you think about Daddy today?' are beginning points that the children may want to use.

Give comfort

If there is no difficulty getting the children to be open, you may find you are called on to give comfort. Holding, cuddling and stroking are activities that help heal your children's hurt. As long as they know they can depend on your loving attention when they are sad, they'll feel safe even while they cry. *It is when they are pushed away with their grief that they feel insecure and scared.*

SUMMARY

- Be prepared to answer the same questions from the children over and over again.
- Don't be afraid of showing your grief initially.
- But do keep a lid on it after the first few weeks. If you need to scream and cry, do it away from the children, or preferably at times when they are out of the house.
- Help your children normalise their feelings by calmly talking about the departed parent and helping them do so too.

4

HOW AGE ALTERS YOUR CHILDREN'S PERCEPTION OF DIVORCE

Divorce academics have been researching the subject of the impact of divorce on children for over thirty years now. We know a great deal more of what to expect in the way of reaction from children aged 0–16 than we ever did in the 1970s when the subject began to be taken seriously. This chapter summarises the results of the research, explaining in easy-to-read sections what children's reactions are likely to be.

Why is this summary useful? It gives you up-to-date information about your own children and if they are playing up, some very feasible explanations as to why. If you understand the symptoms of your children's upset, you will gain a better handle on how to react and how to comfort them.

BABIES

We know little about the effects of divorce or separation on children younger than two or three years old. Very young children do not necessarily suffer through divorce *provided their parents are not in conflict about the separation and about childcare*. However, the most recent research shows that two age groups *are* especially likely to be affected by continuing parental conflict. These are the very young (from 18 months up to three years) and older children (from about three to five years).

Infants

Infants may not understand their parents' conflict but may react to changes in a parent's energy levels and mood. This might show itself by loss of appetite, upset stomach or spitting out food. As the atmosphere cools down, however, so too (hopefully) will their behaviour.

PRE-SCHOOLERS

Children of pre-school age (three to five) experience emotions of shock, anger and depression, but most of them are able to regain their 'cool' within two or three months. It is at this age that children begin to fear that something they have done may be responsible for their parents' separation. They may be afraid of being left alone or abandoned. They may show baby-like behaviour, such as wanting their security blanket or old toys. They may deny that anything has changed or they may become uncooperative, depressed and angry. Although they want the security of being near an adult, they may at the same time be disobedient and aggressive.

A word of comfort to parents. These symptoms may be true of *any* child over the age of two, regardless of their parents' marital status. Think 'terrible twos'! But most children get over it in time.

There is some evidence to show that boys adapt less well to divorce than do girls and that they may need extra support and attention. Much of the newest research makes it clear that if the parents continue to be in conflict even after the separation, then this warfare impacts on the children and continues to wound them. However, many children were helped by the acquisition of step-siblings, and a very intriguing American divorce chat-line for children shows interesting votes of confidence in *caring and involved stepfathers*.

SCHOOL-AGE CHILDREN

Five- to seven-year-olds
By this age, children have developed a better understanding of family dynamics. This comes at a stage when they are also having to experience entry into the school system for the first time, and may complicate a smooth transition. Research has shown up conflicting views of the impact that divorce has on the slightly older age groups. The most positive fact to emerge from the newest material is that many children felt that they were *coping* perfectly well with life two years later and were *doing* reasonably well. This might have been due to the fact that their parents were also happier. The study by Professor Mavis Hetherington of the University of Virginia, which followed more than 2,500 children over thirty years after divorce, noted that some women and girls actually developed greater competence and strength as a result of the divorce.

Seven- to eight-year-olds
Striking differences were noticed between the behaviour of seven- to eight-year-olds and that of nine- to ten-year-olds. Perhaps the most poignant of all was the reaction of pervasive sadness shown

in the younger group. Unlike pre-school-age children in the study, who were able to explain away much of the divorce distress by creating fantasies and using denial, the seven- and eight-year-olds were too old to pretend. They were aware of their suffering but did not know how to relieve it. Since they were unable to analyse their feelings, as the older children could, they appeared immobilised. Most of them were worried about what would happen in the future, even going so far as to worry about whether there would be a home for them. Boys as well as girls did a lot of crying. And the feelings of insecurity showed clearly when they played and also in their constant demands for new clothes or toys. They felt particularly rejected by the departed parent, yet were unable to show anger against their parents.

Only half improved on or maintained their earlier achievements after a year. The other 50 per cent either remained distressed and depressed or even, in a few cases, became worse. The implications of these findings seem to be that seven or eight is just about the worst age for children to see their parents divorce.

These observations were the findings of a detailed survey carried out by Judith Wallerstein in the USA, most recently updated in 2000. In contrast, as we have seen, Mavis Hetherington's research showed that though as many as 25 per cent of children do show some serious emotional damage, the great majority (75 to 80 per cent) showed very little long-term damage and, as adults, were functioning well.

Nine- to ten-year-olds

In contrast to the seven- to eight-year-olds, the nine to ten age group worked hard to master the conflicting feelings they were experiencing. They used denial, avoidance, courage and activity to take charge of their emotions as well as seeking support from others. Unlike the younger group, they did feel shame about the divorce and, as a result, frequently became very angry with their parents. They also felt lonely, partly because they could not see so much of one parent and partly because they felt the parent they lived with was too preoccupied with his or her own difficulties to concentrate on their emotional problems. Fifty per cent of this age group found their progress at school had slackened off, and they did not see their friends so often. However a year later, *most of them had returned to normal in these areas.*

All surveys of children of divorce show that the better adjusted the children are *before* divorce, the more easily they are likely to come through it. However, surveys also show that the parents' mental well-being and behaviour have a direct effect on their children's. The moral of the story is 'clean up the marital act', if only for the sake of the kids!

TEENAGERS

All emotionally healthy adolescents, be they products of divorce or a strong marriage, share one goal in common: that is how to achieve independence from their parents. The 'teenage syndrome' is well known. A previously well-behaved, well-adjusted, pleasant and helpful young person turns overnight into a moody, aggressive, rude and defiant young man or woman. The change in mood, precipitated by sudden fluctuations in hormone levels as a result of puberty, heralds the struggle to break away from the parents who, for the past twelve years or so, have been the main love objects of the young person's life.

An important part of growing up demands a switch of allegiance from parents to a friend of their own age group. By switching their love, they can establish that they are now independent human beings in their own right. The vulnerable single parent, quick to blame the children's dramatic mood changes on divorce, can be reassured therefore that these difficult teenagers are probably not too different from anyone else's difficult teenagers.

However, the surveys do show that this older age group experiences more trouble adjusting to divorce. This is perhaps because the children possess greater levels of anger. In many cases divorce accelerates the natural striving for teenage independence, unfortunately precipitating a premature separation between parent and children that arrives too soon for the children's own emotional maturity.

Wallerstein and Kelly's original study included 21 children over the age of thirteen who demonstrated surprisingly similar reactions to divorce. Each one of them found it a painful event, felt betrayed and angry, and had a sensation of loss. But they did *not* feel responsible for the marriage break-up; having reached a certain level of maturity, they were quite able to see that the break-up was between their parents and was nothing to do with them.

All the teenagers used distancing and withdrawal as methods of protection against emotional pain. They spent more time outside their homes, seeing more friends and making sure that they kept constantly busy. Later on, almost all the children were able to be emotionally supportive to their parents.

In another American study of teenagers and divorce, carried out by David Reinhard (1978), the young people who took part actually agreed that after they had emerged from the initial shock, they had a more mature and realistic view of their parents. They also saw themselves becoming more self-reliant.

The casualties
There were, however, three teenagers in the Wallerstein and Kelly study who experienced a very adverse reaction. Significantly, the reactions of the children in each case seemed to be directly related to their parents' own over-depressed reactions.

1. A thirteen-year-old boy whose mother suffered from a severe hysterical illness and who had a history of suicide attempts became far too protective of her, jealous of her dates, sleepless when she was out, and fearful that she would die of cancer. A year later, his reactions had intensified and he showed no signs of the 'normal' teenage need to break away from his mother.
2. A thirteen-year-old girl had enjoyed an intense relationship with her father although for years he had only communicated with his wife by notes. When the wife divorced him, the family did not see him again, although he paid them regular maintenance. The daughter was particularly struck by his loss, became very depressed and continually worried about him. She lost her friends, played with dolls and much younger children, and slept with her mother. It took her two years to return to a more usual adolescent pattern of behaviour, and this coincided with her mother's remarriage.
3. A fourteen-year-old girl began having sexual adventures when she discovered her father was having an affair. She had fantasies about his sexual activities, threw rocks at his mistress's window, and started sleeping around. Her mother became depressed and took young lovers into the house, whereupon her daughter stepped up the promiscuity, drinking and taking drugs. A year later, nothing had changed.

Since the family background of each of these children was *already* disturbed, it's very possible that they would have had problems even if their parents had not separated. Mavis Hetherington's research indicates this is highly likely.

Specific teenage problems

Even among those teenagers who ended up being helpful and supportive, there were problems along the way. Faced with a lack of parental restraint at a time when they needed rules and regulations to kick against, they reacted by becoming aggressive and anti-social. The fact that their parents were no longer available to give them guidelines on sexual behaviour and outbursts of rudeness was especially confusing.

Conclusion

It does not help teenagers, struggling to sort out confused feelings, to find that their parents have reverted to a state of adolescence themselves. The young people who either benefited from or at least were unhurt by divorce were those who were able to distance themselves from it, right at the beginning. In order to do this, they needed parents who could understand what their children were doing and did not prevent them from behaving in this way.

ENGLISH STUDIES OF DIVORCE

There have been several English research projects in recent years on children and divorce, which confirm many aspects of these two major US studies. Certainly they back up the finding that the more thoughtfully parents handle the separation from the children's point of view (and indeed their own), the better adjusted the children are likely to be.

It helps to realise that if you have children, *you and your ex-partner are still going to be in contact with each other for the next twenty years at least*. If you can understand that in these circumstances it pays to cultivate a civil relationship, this could be of major benefit to your children.

Many of us see divorce as the ending to a relationship. It isn't so final when you are parents! It turns out to be just one stage of your relationship and there may be more to come.

English children

A major difference between the results of the US and the English research is that the English children of divorce did *not* necessarily feel their lives had improved once the shouting was all over and the separation was a fact. Many of them insisted that they were used to the rows and would still have preferred their parents to continue together.

What children want, of course, isn't always possible and doesn't take into account the many small psychological improvements that separation from an unhappy situation brings. Although the children may not be capable of appreciating such improvements now, they may well come to do so later on, as they grow older.

SUMMARY

The difficulty with research of this kind is that it sets itself an impossible task; it attempts to compare what *is* with what *might have been*. Bearing that in mind, the most helpful information to emerge from the recent major studies of the impact of divorce is:

- Children need a great deal of attention paid to them during separation and the years after.
- Children need to mourn properly in their own way.
- This doesn't necessarily mean they will be happy for ever, but it will mean they have learned working methods of how to deal with sorrow and depression.
- It is important not to see divorce as a temporary crisis – *it is a long-term situation that needs as much attention paid to it as does a marriage*.

(5)

WHEN SHOULD PARENTS STAY AWAY FROM THEIR CHILDREN?

The short answer is hardly ever. But there are some situations of divorce or separation that the questions and answers in Chapter 3 do *not* cover – for example, where the deserted parent heartily hates the departed one and honestly feels that it's better never to see him again, or where the departed parent has brutalised the family previously.

A VIOLENT PARENT

However explosive or traumatic the break-up has been, the children's situation in divorce remains much the same whatever the circumstances. They still need contact with both parents. The only cases where it would be wise to avoid the departed parent are those when that parent has been physically cruel (battering, sexually abusive and/or otherwise physically harmful), where you and the children have been in actual bodily danger. In such situations it is better to explain (if indeed it needs explanation) that Daddy/Mummy was sadly a difficult and dangerous man/woman and you are safer living without him/her.

If a partner is pathologically jealous, schizophrenic, a hard-line alcoholic or drug addict, or severely depressed with symptoms of acute paranoia, and has already shown extreme violence, these *are* cases where you and your family need protection and your break-up needs to be explained to the children in terms of 'illness'.

AN UNBALANCED OR OBSESSIVE PARENT

Occasionally one parent has been so difficult to live with that he/she seems unbalanced to the point of insanity. If the parent is suffering from severe mental illness and is an actual danger to you and your children, it is obviously vital to remove yourselves very rapidly from their vicinity and become extremely wary of any renewed contact.

An obsessive father

George Denham, aged 55, has been divorced from his wife for nine years. He is obsessive, depressed and often paranoid. On these grounds, his wife was easily able to obtain total custody and care and control of their three children, especially as her husband's 'eccentricities' were well known to the local authorities. (One of his obsessions was to write letters of complaint to the social services department.)

Unfortunately, Mrs Denham is not a particularly good influence on the children either, because she drinks a great deal and allows her seventeen-year-old son to do likewise. There are constant drunken parties in their home. The eldest daughter got away from the disruption these cause by marrying and leaving the district. The youngest daughter, aged fourteen, would often walk the streets at night rather than go home. She was also poorly clothed, as her mother never had enough money.

Mr Denham, denied any access at all to his children, had managed to keep up contact with his youngest daughter by subterfuge and seems to have a good caring relationship with her. He was very distressed when he found her out on the street one night. He took her straight to his lodgings, made sure she had a room of her own, a decent diet and some new clothes. She in turn felt happier for being looked after, and wanted to stay with him.

Her mother, however, protested strongly to the local social worker and, with no difficulty at all, had the girl placed back under her roof. But she did not change her drunken behaviour, although she had promised to do so.

George Denham is subsequently fighting an almost impossible battle to convince the local probation officer that *he* should have care and control of his daughter. Unfortunately, his reputation as a paranoid obsessive makes this virtually impossible. The result? One very damaged teenage girl. Yet, in spite of his undeniable record of instability, George Denham seems like a good caring parent, better fitted to house the daughter than his ex-wife.

The moral of this story is to keep an open mind. People's mental condition can get better as well as worse.

PLAIN OLD BAD BEHAVIOUR

Some people behave worse with one partner than with another. It is possible that each partner becomes considerably more 'normal' after leaving the other. If this is the case, it might help reassure you about the safety of the children's contact with their other parent. It is probably best explained that together you and Dad/Mum behave badly, but that apart you are both much nicer people.

Extremes of anger

Jane and Ian sent each other to extremes of anger in their marital battles, yet separately they were charming and well-balanced people. Jane eventually met another man who lived life at a less volatile pace. His low-key emotions seemed like a haven to a storm-tossed sailor and she left Ian to set up home with her lover.

As a result Ian went through the divorce syndrome of sorrow, grief, anger and bitterness, but emerged to meet a woman who possessed many of the same qualities as himself, someone who was able to *thrive* on the arguments that made up a stimulating side of Ian's life. Three years on they were quarrelling, but amicably; more for the stimulation than as a result of major disagreement. It would certainly not have occurred to them that these enjoyable tos and fros would constitute grounds for separation. The original husband and wife were able to live perfectly happily provided it wasn't with each other.

Their two children had hated the marital fights and had become quite disturbed by them. Once they were able to see that their parents were happier apart, the children themselves settled down. They were quick to grasp that adults show a variety of behaviour, all of which is normal to those particular individuals. They had no difficulty in accepting the different standards in their two homes, and settled into each amicably.

PROLONGING THE BATTLE

I suspect that many divorces contain an element of disagreement so bitter that it amounts to a type of insanity. Couples often push each other to the edge of this kind of madness, even though in many other ways they are perfectly sane and balanced human beings. Try to remember the sane and balanced bits *as well as* the mad bits when it comes to sorting out the continuing relationship between departed spouse and child.

Driving each other mad

Mary and Colin were temperamentally unsuited. At the start of their marriage they found their opposite characters to be stimulating. But once they had a family, Colin's obsession with efficiency began to seem oppressive to Mary, while Mary's easy-going attitudes nearly drove Colin to despair. The divorce found each trying to nail the other for unreasonable behaviour. Yet each one, when forced to be reasonable about the other by their lawyers, rediscovered the many engaging and 'sane' aspects of their personalities which had made the first years of the marriage happy ones.

'It was about then that I understood the pointlessness of being enraged with Colin,' explains his ex-wife. 'I'd catch myself tearing my hair out in front of the kids and find they were looking at me in astonishment. They simply couldn't see what he had done that seemed so insane to me. I suddenly realised I must appear even more mad than he did.

'After that, I managed to accept that we simply had our differences and that we would be better off living apart. It meant I could explain the break-up more rationally to the kids, which I now realise was very fortunate because Colin could not. He carried on ranting and raving about me. It was lucky for the children that at least one of their parents was able to be nice about the other. It made them feel better.'

Even after separation, back-biting, criticism and hatred of a partner can continue with one angry parent openly and continually expressing such feelings about the other. This sadly can last for years and causes deep anguish to children caught up in their parents' battle.

Acrimony

John and Christina's child, Anna, sadly never knew anything but her parents constantly carping at each other.

'I remember when I was sixteen,' says Anna, 'and my parents had already lived apart for ten years, I suddenly blocked myself off from my mother. After all that time she was still going on about how weak-minded my father was and how his defects had ruined her life. Only the day before, I'd heard my father saying, for the millionth time, how mad my mother was and so how it was impossible to rely on her for anything.

'I hated them for it. I remember feeling quite cold and thinking, from now on I'm not going to listen to either of them. They're incapable of controlling their own lives, so from now on they're not controlling mine.

'My behaviour changed from that time onward. I stopped being patient and tactful with my mother and told her what I really thought. She threw me out and I went to live with my dad and his girlfriend. That was a bit better but I felt badly in need of my own home. So when I met up with the first boy I ever really cared for, he and I squatted in an empty house which we lived in for the next three years.'

It was not the easiest life choice for a sixteen-year-old who was taking her exams and trying to get to university. It is a tribute to Anna's precocious maturity that she slogged away at her school work and got university acceptance in spite of everything. She puts that maturity down to having endured her parents' marital battles for so many years. However, she would be the first to agree that learning through such pain is less than ideal.

LET THINGS SETTLE DOWN BEFORE MAKING MAJOR DECISIONS

If there is some doubt about the departed parent's influence on the children, if you suspect that the children really are being upset or unsettled, it is fair to give the difficult parent a chance to let his/her new home surroundings and his/her feelings time to settle down. Allow the children to visit their parent a number of times before deciding against further access. You should *not make a permanent judgement* on the basis that Johnny has looked upset after just two visits.

Only if you are *absolutely sure* that the other parent is being truly harmful should you think about limiting that access. And I'm hesitant about writing even that because I know many bitter parents will seize on it as an excuse to use their children as pawns.

COME TO TERMS WITH A PAINFUL SITUATION

The fact is that seeing a parent immediately after separation *is* upsetting. *It's probably normal for the children to feel terrible*. Like anyone else, children need time to settle down and readjust. The real difficulty arises when, only after a number of visits, the children seem worse rather than better. These then are the questions you need to ask yourself:

- Is this the wrong kind of access for my children?
- Do they need more of it? Sometimes children are distressed because they don't see *enough* of an absent parent.
- Or do they need less of it?
- Instead of once a month would once a week be better?

- Instead of every other weekend and two nights of the week, would alternate weeks be better?
- Instead of organising visits during each week, would it be better to organise visiting in bigger tranches of time, such as for the school holidays?
- Is there any way in which I could help my ex-partner? It's worth remembering that he/she may not know who the children's friends are, may be unfamiliar with the routines that keep them feeling secure, may not even have provided them with adequate space of their own when staying overnight. If he/she is struggling with a fog of pain and depression, he/she may need advice and support. If you think your ex wouldn't take it from you, try and filter it through friends or relations. Do not use the children to pass emotive messages backwards and forwards!

SUMMARY

- You need to remember it's your *children's* upset you're gauging where visiting is concerned, *not your own*.
- Never deny access except in cases where physical or other harm to the children is likely to occur.
- Parents who behave badly when they're together may be perfectly normal when apart.
- Allow time for the situation to settle down before making any decision to limit access.

6

WHO SHOULD DECIDE ON ACCESS?

SHOULD YOU CONSULT THE CHILDREN?

Younger children naturally will need access decisions to be made for them. Older children should have their opinions sought and taken into account. Access can always be varied.

But be warned. If you feel that cutting down on access would help calm the situation, bear in mind that when men (in particular) are discouraged from visiting their children, they often give up because they cannot cope with the pain this involves. In the UK as many as 50 per cent of fathers lose contact with their families after divorce.

Reduced access for a few months *might* help everyone cool down and give the parent who has left home breathing space, time in which to get his/her new life more organised. But it's risky, worth doing only if everyone is positive that this will result in regular child contact reasonably soon. General advice is to set up and start access immediately so that everyone can take it for granted and a pattern of visiting can be established.

WHEN THE CHILDREN DO NOT WANT TO SEE THE ABSENT PARENT

However, there are times when the children themselves may not want to visit the absent parent. I interviewed several parents and children to hear their individual stories. What became clear as I did so, was that no two stories were the same and that it is therefore very difficult to talk about a right way and a wrong way to organise access. This chapter is devoted to case histories of families where there was not a predictable pattern of visiting.

They chose never to see him again

Carole, Jimmy and Matthew were aged between eleven and fifteen when their father left their mother for a much younger woman. Seeing their mother depressed and unhappy, the children found it impossible to understand or forgive their father and unanimously refused to visit him.

Seven years later they are young adults. Their father remarried and they have a half-brother they've never met. Now the eldest son, Matthew, regrets that he has had no contact. He would like to be friends again but, as he says, 'It's very hard to make that first move when I've rejected him all these years. I just don't think I can do it.'

What a pity that Matthew's parents didn't co-operate better and come up with some version of visiting, even if it were severely reduced. This was a good case for insisting that Matthew and his brother and sister should have visited their father, even if it was only occasionally.

You need to take a long view of contact. Be sensitive to your children's emotional welfare. Mentally stamp on any inclination to use their access as a weapon, but be aware that they may need that other parent at some stage, even if you emphatically do not.

51

Relief

There is even the small possibility that, rather than ask 'Where is Daddy?', the children will heave sighs of relief at getting free of an uncaring parent.

When the children don't notice their father has gone

Jenny and Michael were six and four when their father moved out. They hardly seemed to notice his departure, although their mother, Liz, fell over herself to ensure they all kept in touch. But, as far as the children were concerned, their father was simply sticking to a pattern that had been there all their young lives: he'd never been very involved with them.

They much preferred their new stepfather, who did take an interest and who actively cared for them. When a friend of their mother's asked them if they were sad that their father had left, they were puzzled. It hadn't occurred to them to mind; their father was not someone they had cared about strongly in the first place.

WHEN A PARENT CHOOSES NEVER TO SEE THE CHILDREN AGAIN

What if the departed partner very obviously doesn't care if he/she never has any contact with the child again? The deserted family are presented with a *fait accompli*. As far as they are concerned there is no choice. What is the least hurtful way of dealing with this?

If Dad has formerly been very involved with his family, there's no hiding the fact that his absence will hurt. It's unavoidable. The best moves are to allow yourself and your children time in which to grieve. But make sure they also see how a grown-up can cope with life after Dad. If your children view their mother planning new schemes, organising a new life, and coming up with absorbing and intriguing activities for them too, they will learn from her example.

Helping children become independent

Fascinating clinical work done with parents and children has shown that even the most introverted children can develop good coping techniques provided they are shown them by a parent and given support. Rather than do everything for the children, thus enhancing their feelings of helplessness, the parent should give them projects to achieve for themselves, having briefed them very carefully beforehand and then encouraged them. This way the children learn to overcome their fears. This is a particularly useful method to use with children whose father refuses to have anything to do with the family and who are therefore likely to have issues with self-confidence. Studies have shown this to be an extremely efficient way of helping children progressively grow in confidence.

CHILDREN'S VIEWS ON ACCESS

Research was undertaken in 2000 by the Centre for Research on Family, Kinship and Childhood at the University of Leeds, where 65 children aged between four and seventeen were interviewed to discover their views on post-divorce family life. The results were as follows:

• Most of the children in the study felt it important to them to have both parents involved in their lives.
• For children who moved between households from an early age, moving back and forth was simply routine. However, some children experienced emotional and practical difficulties at some stage.

- Difficulties can arise where parents are hostile to one another and where children are moving between 'war zones'.
- Children are very keen to treat their parents equally and to ensure that they both have a 'fair share', but sometimes this makes it difficult for them to have time with friends.
- Children can see many benefits from the arrangement, including having 'two of everything'. For some, these benefits mitigate the experience of having no settled home.
- Children want to be involved in decision-making about family life, although they do not want to be forced to choose between parents.
- The children who are least happy are those who feel that they cannot talk to their parents about the arrangements and who have no influence on how their time is parcelled out.

SUMMARY

- In general, regular and immediate access needs to be set up and encouraged.
- Children's opinions should always be sought in making decisions about access.
- There are very few circumstances where the children should not have access.
- It's important that both parents encourage the children to keep up with regular activities such as cubs, sport, music lessons or birthday parties, and not to drop them because of what's happened just so they can see their mum or dad.
- Research shows that if access is muddled, unreliable and embattled the children are emotionally harmed. It is important to stick faithfully to arrangements once they have been agreed.

7

THE MONTHS AFTER SEPARATION – HOW TO MAKE ACCESS WORK

It's one thing to carefully work out the children's visiting arrangements and quite another to cope with the practicalities involved. You as the primary parent may be surprised at how difficult you find it is to let the children go. On the other hand, the departed parent who is setting up a new home and living in very different circumstances may feel incredibly swamped by the family the first few times they stay.

PRACTICALITIES

Giving children 'talking support' is part of the adjustment process to living in two homes and needs to be included as one of the practical arrangements parents can provide. This can be done on the telephone and via email (with older children) when visiting is not possible. Other practicalities include:

- a permanent home base
- keeping in touch with familiar friends

- keeping in touch with relations since they offer reassurances that not *every* aspect of life is changing. Divorce is a time when grandparents or perhaps even godparents come into their own.
- making sure the children's schools are informed of what's happening
- making sure school routine remains constant. School can provide a sense of continuity temporarily lacking at home.

WHAT YOUR CHILDREN WILL NEED

My interviews with parents and children threw up several classic requirements that the children will have, regardless of whose home they are in.

1. **A regular pattern of everyday life.** This should be continued if at all possible, since its familiarity provides feelings of security. So if routine consists of breakfast, school, friend home to tea, homework, supper, bath, bed, then that needs to be maintained. Even if the children are staying with the absent parent, he/she needs to keep to a similar pattern. An addendum to this is that it's imperative the absent parent includes the children in his or her new life as normal whenever they visit and does *not* treat them like guests at a birthday party.
2. **Organise the children's social contacts.** Parents' respective roles have changed a lot during the last ten years, bringing dads much more actively into childcare. But it is generally still the mum who organises the family social life. It is normally left to Mum to decide whether or not Joanna goes to play with Christina on Wednesdays, which friends to cultivate on Joanna's behalf and, once she is at school, how many friends and outside activities she can cope with on top of homework and the work

and games she does at school. Life tends therefore to be tough on fathers, because they know less about their children's regular social life and are not used to planning it. They may not even know who their children's best friends are or where they live. *Fathers need to think about these things in advance, and research them*.

3. **Friends.** These are one of the most valuable sources of support a 'divorced' child can have, and it cannot be emphasised too strongly how important it is for children to keep in touch with their mates. This is particularly true of an only child, who has no brothers and sisters to help share the brunt of break-up.

4. **Constancy of access.** Sometimes the children will be painfully affected when they see a parent intermittently, on visits, after they have been used to seeing him/her most of the time. If you are the primary parent this can be the cause of much anxiety. You may feel racked by the dilemma of wondering if the visits should continue. It's certainly wise to think about altering the visits (making them longer or shorter) but equally it's *unwise to end them*. Think how much *worse* it might be if the children don't see the parent at all. In time children get used to meeting and parting, eventually taking it in their stride because they know, as a result of the consistent meetings, *that the departed parent remains there for them*, albeit at their second home. Children are immensely adaptable but it's important to emphasise that the departed parent *must* be consistent about access, must be on time and must *never* forget meetings or cancel them at the last minute. It is when the parent is unreliable, breaking promises, that the children can suffer psychological wounds that scar them deeply and affect them in the long term.

5. **Keeping in touch in other ways.** Sometimes there are physical reasons that make it difficult for a parent to see the

children (he is in Bristol and they are in London, for example). But it is still possible for the absent parent to keep in touch, by telephoning, writing, emailing, sending small presents – all constant and effective reminders to the children that they are still cherished.

6. **Curb your quarrels for the children's sake.** Much of the children's distress stems *not* from the actual separation but from the disturbance they have been experiencing during the previous months or years of their parents' unhappiness. Once the quarrels and discord have been removed from home, they are likely to feel happier. As we have seen, Mavis Hetherington's research found that a majority of children (70 per cent) felt fine two years after the separation and put this down to the cessation of emotional stress. If you and your ex simply cannot help sparking into anger the minute you see each other, you will need to confine your fights to the telephone and make alternative arrangements for picking up and dropping off so that the two of you do not have to meet. If your partner sees the children after school, let him pick them up directly from school. If they are collected at the weekend, arrange for a friend to hand them over at pick-up time. If you have an au pair or a babyminder, let her be the go-between. If Grandma lives nearby, let her do the exchange. And ask your ex to make similar arrangements.

7. **Masculine and feminine role models.** I have heard some of my divorced friends say, 'We're better off without him.' What they actually mean is that they as the former partners are better off. *But their children are not.* Most children need love and attention from both parents. Most children need two parents for role models. Children learn from what parents do, how they do it, and how they react. We discover that their reactions and attitudes differ according to whom they are with. They

unconsciously drink in different sets of values from each parent. They therefore lack the masculine values if Dad disappears from the scene and the feminine ones if Mum opts out of her children's life. (As mentioned earlier, one in eight parents with care of the children is the father.)

RULES FOR SINGLE PARENTS

Perhaps the situation is outside your control, and your spouse has done a runner, never to return. Willy-nilly, your children have an absent parent. What do you do then?

Rule 1. However tempting, **don't run your partner down**. It hurts the kids to think that their mother or father is a swine. There is plenty of time later on for them to work that out for themselves. It is also possible that, given time, your spouse may change his mind about cutting ties with parenthood, will realise that he has made a huge mistake and will want to make up for it. *Separation is an easy time in which to make mistakes*.

Rule 2. It is important for your children to have a **clear image of the absent parent** even if he or she is not physically present.

Imaginary daddy
Angela, aged six, developed a fantasy friend two years after her father disappeared. It is not uncommon for children to invent fantasy friends but Angela told her mother that this friend was Daddy. Daddy, it seemed, was always with Angela wherever she went. If she got into any trouble, Daddy, rather like Superman, would swoop down and rescue her. She would read invisible letters from this daddy, who went away on his travels a lot. He

.../continued

---

would usually write from a faraway place, and the boat trip there and back took such a long time that this explained why they hadn't seen him for ages. Starved of her father, Angela had invented him.

Talk matter-of-factly about your ex-partner, what he/she used to do, what his/her favourite television programme was, how he/she used to hate soap getting in his/her eyes at bathtime, or how they didn't like cheese on toast, just like Junior; it all helps build up a realistic picture of Dad/Mum which is very necessary for your children's mental growth. By feeding them constant information about your ex-partner, you are helping make those children feel whole.

Rule 3. If Dad is the one who has left, **encourage male friends**, brothers or your father to spend regular time in your home. Of course, they won't be the same as Dad, but they will help. Children need both male and female influences. Conversely, if Mum is the departed one, encourage your mother, your sisters, or a housekeeper to take an active part in your lives. (In California, there are kindergarten schools where all the helpers and teachers are men. Ninety per cent of the children attending these schools come from single-parent families; most are living with their mother. The theory behind the all-male staff is that they provide a masculine dimension to the children's lives which would otherwise be lacking.) Parents of older children could encourage them to take part in activities where they'll meet both sexes, such as a youth club. Camping holidays with the school, or with friends, or with holiday play schemes is a method of making new friends *of both sexes*.

ADAPT TO YOUR CHILDREN'S CHANGES

Access arrangements have been made. With some difficulty you settle in to them and feel relieved that the children are happy. Then suddenly the children go and grow older. Now they want something quite different in the way of time with mother *and* father. At around the age of eight, for example, children go through a period of rapid mental growth.

Discovery of reading

Jim, who for years had spent his time being physically very active (he would build with Lego, draw innumerable pictures, thump his younger brother, play exceedingly rough games with friends, and watch television avidly), suddenly discovered reading. Every evening after school he retired to his bedroom where he would cram his head full of comic book heroes, adventure stories and children's detective thrillers.

His mother, who had weekend access to Jim, had up till this time based a great part of their time together on activities to keep Jim interested. Suddenly she found she had time on her hands. And wasn't entirely happy with it. She had enjoyed their former shared activities. Wisely, however, she gave him some space. Instead of insisting, on one occasion, that he helped her bake the cake he had especially asked to make previously, she simply gave him the opportunity to do so. When he refused, she got on with it on her own. She understood that he had moved on. She knew she needed to move on too.

Need for privacy

Everybody needs privacy, and as children get older, that includes them. The parent with access often finds that access time feels artificial – it's quite hard to behave normally. For example, if you are starved of time with your children you may want to spend every precious second with them. It's quite a jolt therefore to discover that your children prefer to withdraw and do their own thing, without you. But please be reassured to know that such changes are normal. *You would have had to adjust to them even if your marriage had remained intact*.

The children's own space

As the children grow older, their need for their own place in the world grows too. In order to develop independence, they need to spend time with their friends. And they should have a space that they can call their own in the home of the parent with access.

A room of one's own

Sarah's father used to find that the best way to make his twelve-year-old daughter feel at home with him at the weekends was for her to know that she had her own place in his house. Sarah had her own room, her own books and a record player. Her friends were as welcome in his house as they were in her mother's home, and he was able to accept that for a large part of their weekends together he might not see her, because she was so busy with the friends.

The children's social life

From around the age of ten the children's wishes about the amount of time they spend in *either* household need to be taken into account. I do not recommend that *every* time they voice a wish it should be granted. But I do think they should be asked what they prefer, and that subsequent arrangements between parents should allow them to feel they have had *some choice*.

Teenagers

Most parents find it helps not to expect much in the way of family participation from teenagers *in either household*. The years before teenagers leave home are times of preparation for eventually living their own life. Don't expect therefore to see much of them, be you Mum or Dad with custody or access, but try not to lose sight of the fact that this *is* an 'in-between' time and there will still be occasions when your nearly adult child will need you very urgently for support. Be prepared therefore to respond to calls for 'emergency' help. Parents of the older child need to remain in the background so that even if they are a resource never used, the children are secure in the knowledge that they are available.

SUMMARY

- Access needs to be kept as flexible as possible.
- As your children grow up, the type of access needs to alter as the children's needs alter.
- If you have been very dependent on your children's company during access you will need to detach a little.
- Even if, as teenagers, your children are out of the home much of the time, be prepared to help them in times of emergency.

8

LEARNING TO LOVE EACH PARENT SEPARATELY

All children have to tackle certain psychological tasks as they mature. Among these is the task of breaking away from one's parents. This can take place:

- in a physical sense (the children move out)
- in a behavioural sense (the children are shockingly rude, thus displaying their 'independence')
- in an emotional sense (the task is to feel separate as an entity, as opposed to feeling merged with a parent's personality).

But the one common denominator these children share is that they are attempting to make the break from parents *who are a couple*. That couple tends to be perceived on child 'radar' as *one being*. The children of separated parents have to tackle an extra psychological task therefore, over and above that of other children – which is to learn to love *each parent separately*. Children of marriages or partnerships that remain intact do *not* have to do this.

It may be this extra psychological task, therefore, that influences the differences in children's behaviour after the break-up of their parents' relationship. With children of a 'middle age', i.e. between seven and twelve, the divided parents may find that their children move heaven and earth to try and get their parents back together again. And such desperate need to see parents still as one entity may get in the way of the children's own mental recovery.

A teenager may become excessively angry with one parent. Often that parent has looked after them for years previously, yet now finds him/herself utterly rejected. This can happen years after the separation and usually indicates that there are problems of rage and anger that were never dealt with properly at the time of the marriage break-up, problems that could be connected to how well the child has managed the extra task of learning to love each parent separately.

HOW TO HELP YOUR CHILDREN SEE YOU SEPARATELY

So how can separating families assist their offspring to see their parents as distinct entities and feel secure in this new view?

1. *Make it absolutely clear from the start that the separation is final and give clear reasons* (however simply put). Children need to know why something happens; they need a logical process to follow and if they get it, they are then able to reason logically that these parents are not going to get back together. Of course it is difficult and painful to do this. It makes everything terribly final and it's hideously sad. But it's necessary.
2. *Offer special time and activities with each parent so that the children can get to know their parents as separate people.* Be prepared, as parents, to give up a lot of extra time to your children during the first months after separation.

3. *Do not vilify the absent parent*. Your children are trying to build up a new picture of this parent as a separate being in his/her own right and it will conflict the youngster terribly if they are taught to demonise this formerly loving person.

4. *Be aware that some children feel they have too much power in the family dynamics*. Some children do actually get between parents and play them off one against the other during ordinary family life. Alternatively they may be able to get one or other parent on their side in an argument or twist a parent around their finger with their desires. This can mean that the children believe they are also capable of reuniting their parents. In such circumstances the parents need to tune into their children's wishful but manipulative behaviour and deflect it rather than give in to it. Attention-seeking behaviour and problems at school may be another method of gaining 'bad attention' – attention that involves drawing the parents back together in order to cope. It's helpful to give all children options so that they feel they have some choice in family circumstances. But the options need to be structured choices that are real possibilities during these changed home circumstances. (See Chapter 12 for parenting methods that work especially well with children of divorce.) It won't help the children to promise them things that you know are not going to happen.

5. *Do not foster the children's fantasies that you will get back together again*. Some parents do this because perhaps they also want it. Explain that although the two of you may well do some things together still, like seeing the teachers, or talking about parenting, nevertheless you are going to live in separate homes from now on. If privately you have a strong desire to get back together with your partner, work on this discreetly. Much better to surprise the children with the good news if and when this should happen. And if it doesn't, then it's helpful and

constructive that the children should have learned they have two separate parents and two separate homes.

6. *Understand that children need to feel they have options in life just as grown-ups do*. This means that they need choices, responsibilities, encouragement, praise, but *not* to have every single wish granted. Life consists of downs as well as ups and the best-adjusted children are those who have learned, with parental support, how to overcome them.

TALKING THINGS THROUGH

Underlying all of the previous points is the value of *discussing* the children's longing sympathetically and clearly. Remember that your task here is to make it clear that your separation is final and that although Mum and Dad may work hard at becoming friends again, they are not going to live together any more.

One thing that helped my children was the explanation that there is a difference between grown-up decisions and children's decisions. This can apply to all sorts of subjects, from the necessity to do homework (a gritty perennial), right through to the choice of schools. While you should certainly listen to your children's wishes and take them into account, at the end of the day you adults are the ones with informed experience and your choices are the ones that should prevail.

A possible conversation

Parent   I know you would love Dad and myself to get back together again. I know that all the changes we have been going through have been really hard on you and that you would love our family to be all together once more. (*You acknowledge your children's strong* *feelings by stating this.*) But I have to tell you that sadly this can't happen. Our decision to live separately is definite. We both want to spend lots of time with you, but it will be separately. We won't be changing back.

Children You might change your mind, Mum. Or Dad might change his! There's always a possibility that Dad will come back, isn't there?

Parent Not really, dear. We are both certain that we don't want to live together any more. Of course I can see that you'd like us to change our minds. It's natural. It's your way of feeling sad about the divorce. And it is a sad thing. But Dad and I will get to be happy separately and then hopefully you will feel a lot better too. (*You have acknowledged your children's feelings and let them see that you understand their longings. You've also informed them that these feelings are part of a process and will improve as time goes by.*)

Children Not sure about that, Mum. (*They look sad.*)

Parent How are you feeling right now, darling? You look very sad. (*This gives the children the opportunity to tune into their own sadness, plus permission to let it out. You are helping them grieve.*)

Although conversations like these are horribly painful, they are also truly helpful. Both children and parents assist the whole difficult adjustment by being able, through talking, to get the sad feelings out and in the open.

Bill's parents

'I can't wait for the two years to be up,' said Bill, aged seven. 'When Pat will move out again.' Pat was his father's girlfriend, destined, little did Bill know it, to become his stepmother. The two years referred to were the remainder of the lease on the family flat, not, as Bill thought in constant moments of yearning, the brief period Pat might be sharing his home.

Bill's parents had explained what was going to happen to the family when they separated. But being only six at the time, Bill hadn't understood properly and the separation had happened so rapidly that no one had noticed he was struggling to make sense of it. Bill had lived with Pat and his father Martin for over a year but still talked incessantly – at least to his friends – about his parents living together again in two years' time.

Fortunately his teacher picked up on this and told Pat and Martin. They and Bill's mother all explained the situation to him clearly but kindly. He was noticeably sad for a while but gradually improved, and when Martin told him that he and Pat were marrying he was genuinely pleased because he felt he was getting a family back again – albeit a different one.

SUMMARY

- Make it clear that your separation is final.
- Encourage your children to spend time with the parent who has left.
- Do not encourage fantasies of reunion.
- Do not blame the absent partner.
- Spend valuable time on giving clear explanations.
- Encourage your children to talk about their feelings.

9

LEARNING TO LIVE SEPARATELY

Perhaps the most difficult thing of all to resolve in the weeks following separation is the ownership of joint possessions. Fights over the family silver, books and records are bad enough, but fights over the children are worse. Children, of course, are *not* possessions, a fact easily forgotten in that awful time of grief.

The children can easily become pawns in a game of 'bargain'. 'If you pay me enough child maintenance, I'll let you see Johnny once a week. If you don't, I don't think you should have any rights to him.' Or 'You're leading this carefree new life now with your new woman and no responsibilities, while here I am, stuck at home with the burden of a child. Why should our son get all his treats from you and none from me because I can't afford them? I don't think you should see him.'

Spare a thought for the children. What about *their* rights? What about eleven-year-old Johnny who is *also* feeling bereft, who needs his father just as much as his mother, and who has no understanding of the financial battle that is raging over his head. It is vital always to arrange separation and access from the children's point of view. It is on this basis that mediation services function. The children's welfare comes first.

'If I hadn't been able to see my father often after the divorce, we'd have lost touch and he wouldn't have been like a father to me,' said one eighteen-year-old boy, whose mother had custody. He was ten at the time of the divorce.

'Seeing my father often is what kept things going; I'd have been very bitter otherwise,' said a sixteen-year-old girl, whose mother had custody. She was eight when her parents divorced.

These are comments from some children of divorce surveyed in Cape Town, South Africa in 1977. One of the questions asked in the survey was which parental behaviours were experienced by the child as most distressing. Over half the children agreed that the thing they found most difficult to cope with was the parents' vilification of each other. Another factor causing distress was the restriction of access that the parent with custody might put on the other parent. A girl of fourteen who was five at the time of the divorce, and whose father had custody, said: 'My father is punishing my mother by not letting her see us, but if he's doing this, *he's punishing me too*' (emphasis mine).

He clung to the kids

Some couples begin their divorce with the best of intentions as far as the children are concerned. 'But as our separation sank in,' says one 34-year-old ex-wife, whose two sons aged five and three live with their father, 'my husband began to realise I wouldn't be coming back, that it *was* truly all over. And the more this dawned, the more it hurt him. He went through a period of sadness, depression, bitterness, extreme anger.

'Although our original agreement had been to share fifty-fifty in the care of our children, he began to make it more and more

.../continued

---

difficult for me to see them without some kind of a scene. I tried hard to disguise this from the kids but it wasn't easy. I was feeling terribly guilty about leaving in the first place, even though I was sure it was the right decision, and of course I was worried about the children all the time.

'As he felt worse he clung to the kids more. They were his only emotional security left. He was terrified that by letting them spend time with me, they'd prefer me to him and he'd lose them as well as me. The sad thing is that by trying to make me out of bounds to them, he endowed me, in their eyes, with a kind of glamour that made them want to see me more than if the access had been easily available and without dramatic meaning.'

SHARED CHILDCARE

There are no hard and fast rules for sorting out shared childcare. In this day and age, it is left to be determined by the parents on the general principle that these arrangements are best shared jointly. (They will of course still have to satisfy the judge, when it comes to divorce, that all arrangements are in the children's interests.)

It's fair to assume, however, that shared care of the children on a fifty-fifty basis is not realistic and that a more practical arrangement is for one parent to be the primary and the other the secondary carer. This tends to mean that the mother has primary care and the father has access. As we have already noted, however, in one in eight families it is the other way round.

There are many traps and pitfalls that the now separated parents can still fall into – often because subconsciously they want to continue the marital battle. One obvious way of doing it, unfortunately, is through the children. What each one may do is perpetuate the existing arguments and differences by using the children as weapons. It hardly needs me to say that this is devastating for the children – horribly damaging.

FOCUSING ON MUM AND DAD

It is important to begin by understanding that *both* parents go through a period of mourning, *not just the partner who has been left*. This can mean that the parent with care sees the offspring as representing a sole remaining security yet also a burden. So this parent (usually the mother) clings to her family, yet feels continually under immense strain. She may be snappy and bad-tempered with the children, yet find it difficult to let them out of her sight. Ironically, by letting go, by allowing them to visit friends, grandparents *and their father*, she will help the children and therefore herself in the long run.

Dad's life

Meanwhile, the father's life has undergone many changes, not all of them welcome, despite his so-called freedom. His accommodation may be uncomfortable, he is probably doing his own cooking, cleaning and laundry – and, worst of all, for the first time in years he's alone.

Though he welcomes his children, they inevitably remind him of happier family occasions and of what he's lost. Some dads, in this situation, focus too intensely on the children. 'He used to just sit and watch Thomas, who was only fifteen months old then,' said one mother. 'It got to the point where he didn't move out of his flat on the weekends he had Thomas. Just wanted to gaze at the child. Of course, Thomas became appallingly bored and not a little disturbed. He needed something more normal.'

Although it is very understandable that the father should give his kids concentrated attention on the relatively brief occasions he may now see them, he should try to remember that a young child needs to use up its energy and gets very bored if there is nothing to do.

Dad's sense of loss

The parent who has moved out may find the sense of loss over his children so intense that he needs to distance himself from them so that he is not constantly reminded of that loss. He may even misguidedly decide not to see the children at all. But I must emphasise again that children *do need continued contact with their departed parent.* So, the urgent message to Dad is that, if he can possibly manage it, the passing of time will help heal the loss (though it may never entirely disappear). The equally urgent message is that he needs to be very adult himself and stick out the pain, rather than cut himself out of his children's lives, a move which he may bitterly regret later and which would cause needless pain to his offspring.

Depression

Divorcing parents suffering from depression may find it difficult to cope with the stuff of everyday life – chores such as housework and cooking. So the children may find themselves struggling through a mess of debris at their mother's house, or visiting a bleak new pad which their father hasn't had the energy or the inclination to turn into a home.

Unfortunately these manifestations of depression become ammunition for embittered spouses.

'Is it wise for him to see so much of the children when he can't even look after himself?' she accuses.

'Won't it hurt the children to be in the care of someone who seems so unbalanced?' he demands.

If each parent could manage to recognise that his/her depression is a symptom of mourning, he/she might be able to make allowances for it as well as suggesting methods of overcoming it – talking to a counsellor being one option. Only in extreme cases would drug therapy be appropriate.

ACCESS PROBLEMS THAT MAY EMERGE

Who is responsible for the children's welfare?

It can be very hard for the secondary parent to accept that the primary one now bears the main responsibility for child-rearing. This involves recognition and acceptance that the mother (usually) now has the legal and emotional duty to raise the children according to *her standards and her philosophy*. When a dad cannot accept that this responsibility *is no longer his*, he makes the potential for conflict over the children far worse.

Such an acceptance doesn't mean he has to change *his* standards. *Children are quite capable of realising that different homes demand different behaviour.* But it does mean that a father *should not directly challenge what the children are being taught by their mother.*

How to avoid responsibility conflict

It is better to say, for example:

'I know at home your mother insists you're in bed by six thirty. But here we have a rather later bedtime. Your mother and I have different ideas about this.'

rather than

> *'Six thirty is a ridiculously early hour for bedtime. Your mother's a fool to insist on it. Of course you should be allowed to stay up later.'*

All of this kind of conflict heightens the children's distress. Difference of opinion over bedtime is, of course, only a minor problem compared with, say, schooling and religion – major debating points affecting the entire trend of a child's life.

Talk about your children – communicate!

It is obviously best if parents can talk to each other to try and resolve differences, but if this is impossible, the parent without custody must accept that these decisions are no longer his. Once he can do so, the tensions between parents will simmer down and the children, both victims and spectators, will be able to breathe more freely.

Talking on the telephone

I used to discuss childcare decisions with my ex-husband on the telephone. I would choose a time when he was in the office and therefore in a businesslike frame of mind. We were able to talk in this atmosphere without getting into angry fights. We used to work out together what was best for our boys. We tackled small things like the right time for bedtime but we also considered bigger subjects such as our boys' options if something went wrong at school. And we did this regularly, *as often as was necessary*, which might be twice a week but might also be twice a day! I'm convinced it was this regular conversation that assisted the two of us eventually to become friends again. If email had been invented I suspect that would have been even better.

Accept that children prefer their primary home

Sad though it may feel, the father with access needs to accept that his children's life will revolve around their mother's home because it is *their* home. This means that the children unconsciously make choices that ease their life in their primary home. So, for example, if when the children are given a free choice of which home they want to spend time in, they tend to choose their mother's, Dad should not back-bite or complain. *It is natural that the rhythm of the children's lives should be centred on their main home and it will hurt them if an issue is made of it.*

Accept that they may need to spend more time with Dad – not less

Sometimes children seem emotionally insatiable during the time they spend with Dad – *they can't get enough of him*. One way of toning down such an intense atmosphere and making it more normal is to *extend* the time the children spend with that parent.

It is difficult to cram into three hours the love and affection children might otherwise express over the luxury of a week. But if they know they can spend *more* time with their dad, they can gain a more relaxed attitude to these visits.

It is the primary parent, though, who has to allow these extra hours. A mother, with fears of losing her children's affection, may find this a hard decision to come to. If, however, she can accept the idea that *the more relaxed the visiting is between children and father, the more secure the children are likely to feel with her*, this might help her to be more generous.

Hate on both sides

It helps no one if the children's real need to see their father is viewed as fuel for warfare. 'He encourages our daughter to be upset, because it makes him feel more wanted,' says one mother,

.../continued

---

sore about the amount of time she is without her child. 'I consider that he is an emotionally disruptive influence on Jennifer's life. He shouldn't see her so often.'

It is hard to tell how much of this is true and how much of it is confused emotion on the part of Jennifer's mother. *Either way, the result is conflict for Jennifer*. Her parents would benefit from a trip to a child guidance counsellor or mediation service. And Jennifer's preferences should also be considered (although not allowed to dictate).

WHAT THE RESEARCH SAYS ABOUT ACCESS

Wallerstein and Kelly, in their 1974 survey of sixty families affected by divorce, reported that it was *in families where the children were allowed easy and flexible access to their non-custodial parent that the children were best adjusted*.

Let the children see enough of you

One of the complaints made by the children in the first research interview was that they were not able to see *enough* of the parent with access. It became clear that feeling helpless and unable to alter this was hurtful. In sharp contrast were those children who were able to *bicycle between their parents' homes*, consequently feeling in control of the situation and therefore a lot happier.

See your children regularly and faithfully

Erratic visiting times and frequently broken promises were regarded as being especially destructive to the young ego. Five- to six-year-olds, coping with this, managed their distress by holding on firmly to their fantasies of a loving, caring absent parent, even when this was patently untrue. Seven- to eight-year-olds received the most visits from the parent with access, very possibly *because they asked for the visits most*. Nine- to twelve-year-olds reported the most erratic visiting, frequently with no contact at all. They didn't hesitate to let the absent parent know their angry feelings and although they may have had good reason to be angry, there was a knock-on effect to their anger in that it probably made diminished contact worse!

Adolescent independence

Adolescents visited more often than the nine- to twelve-year-olds although not much more. But their less frequent visits tied in with their teenage needs to be independent, to have lives of their own and also to be more casual in attitude.

Visiting in a group

Younger children tended to visit in a group with their other brothers and sisters. Older ones were more likely to go to the absent parent on their own. When the younger brothers or sisters visited separately, this was often the cause of hard feeling, occasioning much envy and distress. Feelings of deprivation and of being cheated were heightened. *Separate visits for youngsters only worked well if the parent was able to give similar individual attention to each child in turn*.

Improve the access

At Wallerstein and Kelly's first interviews many of the non-custodial parents hadn't realised how much their visiting patterns affected the children. One of the results of the first interviews was that by the time of the second interview, a year later, many parents had deliberately stepped up the number of visits, making them longer as well as more frequent. *Even the parents who had been doubtful about contact with their offspring reported the new family life as being much happier*.

A new home life

At this stage of the separation new social patterns had emerged in the new homes. The parents with access had developed different relationships with their children, assimilating the children more into their own new lifestyle and developing social activities and friends with whom the children were included.

Improved relationships with Dad

What became clear was that this newly formed relationship between access parent and children possessed great potential for increasing closeness. In most cases the father was the one with access and very often the access gave them intimate time with their offspring that they had *never enjoyed before*.

The pain of being ignored

Saddest of all were the families where the parent had ceased visiting and *yet lived nearby*. This created (for the children) a most painful psychological dilemma. As Wallerstein and Kelly reported: 'In our experience the unvisited child feels that he, the child, is unworthy and unlovable. The seriously diminished self-esteem that eventuates is very difficult to dislodge, even in extensive psychotherapy. As the child approaches adolescence, he becomes more capable of understanding and objectifying the father's problem in sustaining relationships. *For many children that under-standing comes late, after many years of anguish and nagging doubt*' (emphasis mine).

Frequent visits

Wallerstein and Kelly went on to say that there were surprisingly *few* instances where frequent visits were detrimental to the child. Even when the non-custodial parent was unbalanced or disturbed, their personal disturbances did not necessarily spill over into the visiting relationship. (The only notable exceptions where visiting placed the children at risk were those – of course – where a child was being sexually misused, or where the child was being exploited as a housemaid.)

You are always important as a parent

Wallerstein and Kelly concluded their report by observing that even when a parent is absent or not fully present, he or she *can still maintain a significant and tangible presence in their children's lives*.

OTHER CHILDREN'S STUDIES

Other studies where children have been canvassed for their opinions regularly report that:

- They do not feel their *own desires to be taken into account enough*.
- Where there have been court orders strictly defining their access to their absent parent, children resent the rigidity of this, often wanting to bend it according to their feelings at the time and, since they are never able to, resenting the fact that these feelings apparently don't count with their nearest and dearest.
- A particularly positive value attributed to the non-custodial parent is that of helping the children *come to terms with the remarriage of the parent who has care of them*.
- In general the studies conclude that children and absent parents have great potential for *increasing closeness and continuing affection*.

SUMMARY

- It is difficult for the parent with custody to get used to taking all the decisions at home.
- It is difficult for the parent with access to realise that he no longer has control over his children's lives.
- Games of blame and possessiveness should be kept out of the children's lives.
- Parents might ultimately help themselves as well as their children by talking to or emailing each other.
- If the parent with custody tries to be generous and the parent with access tries to be gracious, they can go a long way towards improving the after-divorce relationship.
- Remember the mantra: co-operation not conflict.

(10)

HOW WILL YOUR LOVE LIFE
IMPACT ON YOUR CHILDREN?

Most of us enjoy sex and many go so far as to say that sexual instinct shapes our entire lives. However great or small a part sex actually plays, there is one indubitable fact. When you're not getting enough of it, it becomes a problem!

When you have to do without it, you miss it. You miss it partly for its own sake and partly for the sense of value it bestows upon you. You find yourself back in a singles situation and yet . . . you're not single. There are one or more adorable little people who tag along with you, apt to break into the proceedings just when you are having a cuddle with your new partner, screaming for attention at *the* most inconvenient time.

What should you tell the children?
And then there's the moral dilemma. Should the children know you have a new friend? If it *is* all right for them to know, just *how much* should they know? It's one thing dangling a nice steady friend in front of them, but it's quite another when you're dating five people in one week or a new friend every fortnight. Should they be let in on any of this or none of it?

Privacy issues

Will the children suffer if they learn the truth? Or will they remain totally unaffected? If they discover you have locked the bedroom door one Sunday afternoon, what are they going to feel? Come to that, what are *you* going to feel, hearing their shrill little voices from the fleeting luxury of the ex-marital bed? How important is your privacy? Are you entitled to *any*? And what about the children's space? Is that being trespassed upon by including Mummy's/Daddy's friend at the breakfast table next morning?

These are incredibly tricky issues and there are no hard and fast answers. Each family seems to demand its own solution. Men and women have different methods of coping with a new sex partner (or partners). These range from being flagrantly open to having nothing to talk about because they remain resolutely celibate. The answer for most of us, I imagine, lies somewhere in the middle.

DO'S AND DON'TS

There are a few general principles, such as:

- Take your time over bringing a new partner into the family. Introduce them gradually.
- Don't move a new partner in the minute your marriage has ended. This is too fast for the children to get used to the new way of life.
- Don't have sex in front of your children. (*This shouldn't need to be spelled out, but . . .*)
- Don't be afraid of a lover being openly demonstrative to you, e.g. cuddling you. (*Sometimes this shows that you are valued in ways that your former partner may not have shown for a very long time. It doesn't hurt children to know that their parent is attractive and cared for.*

In order to give you an idea of the diversity of solutions found by separated mums and dads wanting a love life, the rest of this chapter contains personal stories. They offer a broad picture of how a new love life can affect the children of the house. Some of these parents probably harmed their children. Many others developed very mature relationships with their children, especially when the children grew older. In some cases grandparents were enormously helpful in becoming extra 'parents' in order to give their son/daughter a romantic break. I have passed no judgements on any of the following individuals, however extreme their story. Read on and make up your own mind!

MARSHALL

Marshall is a 42-year-old accountant who is the primary carer of his three teenage children. Six years ago, when his marriage broke up, the children were all under eleven. Marshall's strong Christian beliefs influence his lifestyle. He is a just man, although passionate to a point where sometimes his views become over-intense. He puts the spiritual welfare of his children above material welfare but also believes in giving them as much independence as is possible.

When his marriage ended, Marshall's strong sense of morality dictated that he should provide the children with an alternative mother as soon as possible. With this end in mind, the next time he fell in love he promptly moved his girlfriend in.

'The sex was wonderful,' he said, 'but nothing else was. I'd expected far too much from her. She was twenty-five, a very nice person, but she found the children a struggle. After two years of trying to make it work, we parted in an almighty explosion.'

Marshall's choices

'Apart from leaving me distressed, it posed some tricky questions. *I did not think it would be good for the children to go through that again.* I wasn't prepared to live with someone again for some time, but I *am* easily attracted. The trouble is I don't like the idea of going to bed with someone, yet excluding her from the rest of my life. I found myself in a real dilemma. As I saw it, I was faced with the choice of disliking myself by using women in outside sexual relationships, disturbing the children by repeating the first mistake, or doing without sex at all.

'I should say that during my relationship with my girlfriend, the children, to my surprise, adjusted very easily to her — I now know they took an exceedingly sanguine view of my emotional and sexual needs. Little does one realise how well one's children know one! I have always been open in my discussion about sexuality and in my reading matter concerning sex. The children took our relationship and explosive break-ups in their stride, bless them, and pulled me through the crisis. But that didn't alter my feeling that it would be a bad idea to subject them to that all over again.'

Celibacy

'What eventually happened was that my sex life wound down gradually. I didn't artificially cut sexual possibilities from my life. I love women and, in the event, did become sexually involved with a few more. But I learned to live happily on my own (without a woman, that is), to conquer loneliness, living for each day. In the end I survived without a woman at all and, most recently, without *any* sex at all.'

Marshall's present views on sex

'I don't know what people make of me and I don't really care very much. Most women seem intensely curious and not a little puzzled.

I'm aware that it's a highly attractive set-up to many of them, though the slightly cautious ones interest me more and I'm not *desperate* for a mate. Yet the company of women is one of the joys of my life. I am content to hope they like me. I really don't feel I have anything further to prove, and I've a sneaking suspicion that single-parenthood was the best thing that ever happened to me.'

DON

Don has joint care of his young sons (aged four and six at the time of divorce). They live with him most of the time and when he was first divorced he employed a full-time housekeeper to help care for them. His house is designed so that his bedroom is on the ground floor, near to the front door, while the children's rooms are on the top floor near to the housekeeper's room. This ensures a certain amount of privacy for Don.

Don's need to date
'Immediately after my marriage break-up I found myself dating every female I could lay hands on. I think I was trying to prove to myself that I was still attractive, as the departure of my wife had given me serious doubts.

'It got slightly embarrassing bringing a girl home after I'd done it once or twice. The children would interrogate them. Are you going to stay here with our Daddy? Do you know Daddy's other girlfriends? Do you know Betty, Hetty and Letty? Only the strongest women survived that.'

Childish interruptions
'Then came the dilemma of the sexual side to things. I managed to be private with my girlfriends. But in spite of this I felt most

uncomfortable making love with them at home. There was always the possibility of that little rap on the door from one of the kids, "Daddy, Jimmy's fallen out of bed and is crying," and although I didn't particularly care what the housekeeper thought, I was aware of her presence too.'

The mornings after

'Then there were the mornings after. What to do with my girlfriends? I'm inhibited, a lot more so than my children, probably. In any event, I didn't want the children to know these women had spent the night. My fear was that one of the boys would barge in and see a strange head on the pillow where his mother's had once been. So I used to subject the poor women to the most awful subterfuges.

'If I really liked a girl I'd stand her outside the front door at half past six in the morning and pretend she'd dropped in for breakfast on her way to work. The children swallowed that one. If I wasn't that keen, I'd whip out of bed at two in the morning and drive her home. It didn't please her and it certainly didn't suit me. I needed all my sleep in order to cope with an exacting job and two lovely but demanding little boys. On top of this, I can see now that I was very depressed. Everything had gone wrong at the same time. My wife had left me, my previous job had folded and I had had to move house, so things were tough.

'Needless to say, all this standing outside the front door at six thirty a.m. didn't exactly endear me to the favoured women friends and I found myself doing without them rather smartly. Which was hard when I really liked them. However, I stuck to my principles because I felt strongly that the kids needed safeguarding. Perhaps I thought they would think they were losing my affection by seeing me give it to someone else. In any case, I wasn't taking any risks.'

Getting much closer to the boys

'This went on for the best part of two years. One good result was that I developed a very warm and close relationship with my kids. We spent a lot of time together. I became more involved with them and much more appreciative than I had been before their mother left.

'The tireless dating slowed down after the first six months and I took things (and women) rather easier. When I met the first one who appealed to me in every way it suddenly seemed perfectly natural to include her in my life. She understood my inhibitions about our sex life – indeed, she shared them. Suddenly I lost mine. I didn't mind if the boys did see me with her. I was so proud of her I wanted them to be, too. I was very happy for them to see me with her day and night.'

The right woman

'After we'd known each other for four months she moved in with us. Although there was never any pretence that she was their mother, she immediately became their stepmother in spite of our not being married. She just naturally merged into our family, which was another reason why I cared for her so much. After we'd lived together for two years we married. She was the first woman I was happy to be found in bed with!

'Looking back, I suspect I need not have been nearly so concerned for the children. I think they knew a lot of what was going on anyway. But I didn't want to take the risk of hurting them more.'

BRENDA

Brenda's baby, Matthew, was eighteen months old when her husband left her. Unable to afford her flat, she moved back home to her parents. Living conditions were crowded so Matthew shared her room. They continued to live there until Matthew was thirteen, when Brenda remarried.

'I've always been an independent woman,' she says. 'I didn't want to get remarried just to provide a father for Matthew. I could have done that several times over. I wanted to marry to please me or not at all. But all the same, Matthew had to come into it. It would obviously have been pointless marrying someone who was at war with my son. Which meant that an awful lot of men crossed my life until it finally happened.'

Brenda's 'bed-sitting room'

'And sex was one hell of a problem. There was no way I wanted Matthew to see a succession of "uncles" in and out of my bedroom. Even though I was able to get a lot of privacy, my parents were still around. I used my room as a bed-sitting room on the nights I entertained, and Matthew would move his bed into my parents' room.

'But even when my motives were innocent, which was most of the time, I'd feel quite hot under the collar if ever I did have a young man around because I'd be wondering all the time what my mum and dad thought. I am quite a sexy girl so it was all rather uncomfortable. I don't think anyone wants their parents to think of them as sexy. I didn't anyway.'

Right man for Matthew, wrong man for Brenda

'Most of the time, if I was dating, I'd go to the fellow's place. I was fortunate in having my parents as built-in babysitters and often Matthew wouldn't even know there was someone in my life.

'There was one man, though, who was very good with children. I did bring him home and Matthew, who was six at the time, adored him. They struck up a wonderful friendship and Peter would just cart Matthew off for whole days on outings. I was very tempted to marry him because of it. But I withstood the temptation. He was very nice but he really wasn't right for me. Even after he and I were no longer going out, he still saw Matthew occasionally. He was a really nice man.'

Exceptional grandparents

'The reason I was able to last out living with my parents for twelve years was that they did manage to let me have a great deal of privacy, and they provided stability for my son. His grandad was a father figure to Matthew, for which I shall always be grateful, and my mother was very patient and helpful to both of us. Of course, it wasn't ideal. I often longed for my own flat but the disadvantages of that would have been hideous.'

Taking things gradually

'Andy started off like any of the others, a good friend whom I also had sex with at his place. I'd known him for years, from before Matthew was even born. But it wasn't till Matthew was ten that we slowly but surely fell in love. I was very happy to introduce him to my family. He and I took Matthew on several holidays where I made no secret of the fact that I shared a bedroom with him. But back home, he still didn't stay. It just didn't seem right. I got into the habit of staying with him a couple of nights a week and my mother would take Matthew to school on those days. He knew where I was, of course. He had Andy's phone number and phoned me there once or twice.'

'Then one summer holiday we all had to get up at the crack of dawn to catch a ferry and Andy stayed overnight with us. He slept with me and Matthew slept in the living room. It seemed the natural thing to do at the time. But thinking about it afterwards I realised that it was a breakthrough. Everyone had accepted him, and so had I. And that's when we decided to marry.'

FRANCESCA

Francesca found herself in a similar position to Brenda. Her second husband left her when their baby was tiny. She moved back into her father's flat when Timothy was a year old. She was fiercely determined never to marry again, and equally determined to pursue her career in the civil service, even though it was extremely difficult to do so when the baby was young.

'There was no way I was going to be celibate,' she says, 'I love sex although I'm very cautious about long-term relationships with men. That's mostly because I've been unlucky with the men I've picked. They've been marvellous lovers, but lousy husbands.'

Finding privacy

'It quickly became apparent that I was going to need some privacy. I couldn't take a succession of lovers back to my father's flat. To begin with, I borrowed a friend's flat, which I was able to use during the day. At the time that suited me well since I was having a torrid affair with someone who worked quite near me and we used to spend every lunch hour in the luxury of my friend's pad.

'Later on, when I was earning a lot more, I continued to live with my father but also rented my own little bachelor flat. I made no secret of doing so. My son by that time was fourteen and understood the value of privacy. Indeed, he occasionally stayed in the little flat too.'

An important grandfather

'My father was quite accepting of my independence by then, although he'd given me a tough time in earlier days. He put up no argument about my pad, partly I suspect because he was very anxious that I shouldn't remove Timothy from his home. He has cared for him in his own funny way, and has supplied a fatherly influence, which I know has been good for Timothy.'

A mature sixteen-year-old

'I can talk to Timothy about anything and that includes my love life. He's sixteen now and is already studying for A levels. There haven't been any girls in his life yet because he's been working so hard academically that there hasn't been time for any.

'His break with us will come when he goes to university, which won't be long now. He's turned out to be a very good-natured, well-balanced individual. He's loving and understanding and will make some girl a wonderful old man.'

JACKIE

Jackie was 31 when her husband left, and she had three small sons to bring up. Jackie retained the family home and a fixed income for a limited number of years.

'As soon as Mick had moved out, I went out to places where I made quite sure everyone knew I was available. I really needed men friends to prove to myself I was still attractive. I went a bit mad at first, going from one to another. But then I went on holiday to Majorca and met up with a man I fell passionately in love with.

'There were an awful lot of things wrong with him – still are. He drinks, and he's married. But he's also very rich and his job entails travelling around the world so he is able to get to England a lot.'

The quality of sex

'While I was married I'd never given a thought to the quality of my sex life. I'd just taken it for granted. I'd known Mick since I was sixteen and our sex was always good. It hadn't occurred to me it wouldn't be the same with everybody. But it wasn't. One of the reasons I slept around so much to begin with was that either the men were unsatisfactory lovers or I froze up with them. Either way, it wasn't right. So when I met Erik and the sex was wonderful, that hooked me. It didn't matter that he was unsuitable husband material. I loved him.

'When he was in England he would stay with me. There was absolutely no secret about the fact that he shared my bedroom. (I'd never brought anyone else back home, mind you.) My two-year-old was an exceedingly poor sleeper and had got used to sleeping with me by then. He didn't take too kindly to finding Erik usurping his place. The result was that Ollie would crawl in with us. We'd wake to find him fast asleep, kicking us while he sucked his thumb.

'But he did become a hazard to our sex life. He seemed to be there in bed with us all the time. We never really had a moment's privacy.'

Sharing a partner

'The years went by and the relationship with Erik continued. It was a stormy and passionate one. He behaved appallingly when he was drunk but like an angel when sober. One minute he was going to divorce his wife and marry me. The next minute he was back with his wife again.

'I went over and stayed near him in Majorca several times. His wife and I eventually met and managed to make friends. United in the face of the common enemy. He'd mucked both of us around so much we were in very similar situations. He has effectively ended up by having two wives. She has got used to me, and I have accepted that he obviously isn't going to leave her. As long as we both get a fair amount of his time, I can cope. The big threat would be if a third lady came on the scene.'

The effect on the children

'How has all this affected the children? It's been going on a long time now, about eight years in all. My eldest was ten when I met Erik, and he was already very mature. He'd had to be. I'd leant on him heavily when Mick quit.

'The middle child I've never got on well with and he is at boarding school, which has effectively removed him from much of the drama.

'The baby has never really known any different. He's spoilt, I grant you that. But he's always been rather special, a souvenir of my husband whom I loved very much. I hadn't wanted Mick to go. But on the surface at least Ollie seems a normal little boy to me. He's boisterous, has got lots of friends and likes all the things that other kids do. He lives on a diet of fish fingers and ice cream, rides his bicycle all over the neighbourhood and does reasonably well at school. He's a lovely kid.'

CAROLINE

Caroline and Brian have been legally separated for five years. Seven-year-old William lives half the week with his mother and the other half with his father. There have been two main love affairs in Caroline's life since she left Brian.

'I'm a one-at-a-time girl,' she says. 'If only the guys had worked out well I'd have been very happy to get married. Unfortunately, neither of them did.'

Both men in their turn moved into Caroline's home, and so for the years they spent there each effectively became William's stepfather. 'He didn't think much of the first guy but was very keen on the second.

'But William has a good sense of perspective. He sees so much of his own dad that he never thought of either of my lovers as anything other than Mummy's friends. His dad and I are the central figures in his life.'

Sexual discretion

'Of course he's seen me in bed with my live-in lovers in the mornings. It would have been impossible to avoid and in any case there didn't seem to be any reason for doing so. When you live with someone, going to bed with him is part of that relationship and I wouldn't want William to think anything else.

'Now, however, things are a little different. I'm dating four guys at the moment and am going to bed with two of them. So far I've managed to either stay at their places or to have them over on the evenings and weekends that William is with his dad. As none of them is really important to me yet, I don't want William to see them coming and going. I don't want William to grow up thinking of me as some kind of a scarlet woman, even if that's what I am.

'I believe there's a place for discretion in one's sex life and this is definitely it. I also think I'm entitled to some privacy. I wouldn't expect William not to have a love life when he's older, but I don't especially want it thrust under my nose and I don't suppose he would want that either. He's an intelligent little kid and we have a healthy respect for each other.'

VALERIE

Valerie and Jonathan have been divorced for eight years. Before their marriage broke up they had led an extremely varied sex life, which included group sex parties and threesomes. Jonathan is a chartered surveyor and Valerie a successful author. You need to be fairly uninhibited to take part in group sex activities and Valerie's lack of inhibition spilled over into her life after the divorce.

Formal introductions

She was not backward in inviting attractive young men home to stay the night and there was no question of sneaking them out at three o'clock in the morning. Her children in the early days would come into her room to say hello when they woke up. Greatly to the incumbent's surprise, the children would be formally introduced and would shake hands with him. But there was no need for any confusion he might have felt because the children really did accept the presence of their mother's lovers without batting an eyelid. They would chat to their mother and would then go on down to breakfast.

A cynical son

The children are now aged eighteen and sixteen. 'My son has adopted a half humorous, half cynical attitude towards me,' says Valerie. '"Oh, mother and her sex life," he's been known to cry. "The well-known sex maniac."

'He accepts my lovers as a way-out part of my character. Just because I have zany ideas doesn't mean he's the same. He isn't. He's a tolerant, easy-going young man with an intelligent sense of humour. He's just about to go to university where I think he will be immensely successful.

'This last summer has seen the rise of *his* own love life. He fell in love with a girl of the same age and, I'm glad to say, has been quite happy to bring her to our house where I assume they have made love. He has his own room, which he now uses as a bedsit, and what goes on in there is his business and no one else's.'

A responsible daughter

'My daughter is two years younger and still a little girl in many ways. She spends hours in front of the mirror trying on my clothes. She goes to the local youth club with her girlfriends and is rather giggly about boys. My lovers are on totally different planes to her little boyfriends. She's still a virgin although she is reluctant to talk about it. But we have communicated most decidedly about contraception. *She* decided to go on the Pill about three months ago even though there is no immediate need for it. Both her father and I drummed into her the importance of taking responsibility for your own body and for any resulting offspring. And she has done so. So good for her!

'For the past three years I have mostly dated one man. He spends a great deal of time with us although he also has his own flat. In many ways I'd like to remarry but his age deters me. He's about fifteen years younger and it seems such a big gap. But I've changed. I don't have the energy for such frenzied goings-on as I used to. If Paul and I are still together in two years' time maybe I'll think seriously about marriage.'

JOHN

John is 22 and was brought up by his mother, a single parent, in a suburb of Birmingham. 'Mum was a rebel of her time,' he says. 'She did what she thought was right, which was to have long-drawn-out affairs with men who seem in retrospect to have been totally unsuitable. She declined to remarry, even though one of her suitors was a terrific fellow whom I adored. I've always missed having a father around. I can remember passionately wishing I'd got a father like the other kids.'

Mum didn't marry the man I really liked
'She didn't bring a lot of men to our home, but I was aware they were around. When I was thirteen she seemed to be out an awful lot at night. I didn't like it. I didn't like being left on my own but I didn't particularly want her to bring her men back home. I suppose I was

difficult and resentful after her affair with Tony fell through. Tony was the one fellow she did bring home to stay. He lived with us for nearly two years and I liked everything about him. Yes, of course, he slept with my mother. Who else would he have slept with?

'I do not subscribe to my mother's theories of freedom and liberation. She can call it what she likes – I call it sleeping around. She did bring someone else home after she bust up with Tony. It wasn't the sex I resented so much as the assumption that this stranger ought to be welcomed by me. I didn't want her "modern" ideas of living. I wanted a father. I wanted Tony.

'I suppose I haven't really forgiven her. I left home as soon as I could afford to and live very differently now. I'm going out with a nice girl I met at the Young Conservatives and we are saving up to get married. I think my mother is upset by the fact that I hardly see her now. But since she's just gone off on her fourth pilgrimage to India with some long-haired freak who's young enough to be my brother, I can't believe she's grieving too badly.'

CONCLUSIONS

This collection of case histories demonstrates what a poor idea it is to generalise about sexual 'norms' and the 'right way' to conduct a sex life. Every one of these interviewees coped with sex and romance differently.

A pattern to dating

A common pattern among single parents consists of:

- beginning single life with many lovers
- building up self-confidence through these lovers
- eventually settling down with one special partner.

Privacy

For both parent and children, this emerges as vital. Most of the parents insisted the children were more at ease with their new sex life than the parent was. Not all did so, however. And the young man who had adopted a way of life totally contrary to his mother's may be an example of a situation where the mother has missed her child's reactions with spectacular failure. It's a pity, because if resentments or understandable unease can be routed out and dealt with early enough, the parent's sex life is much less likely to become a focus for the children's distress.

Avoid your children feeling rejected

If the children are insecure because their parents have separated, their parent's new lover may represent a threat. They may feel rejected by their parent's new interest. Show them in little ways that this isn't the case. If the lover gets a lot of cuddles, make sure the children do too.

The well-balanced child

If you can remember that your child is not likely to be as shocked as you think, perhaps that will enable you to proceed with a little less tension. It is healthy to have a good sexual and emotional life. Starting a new relationship may mean settling down one day with a loving and caring partner. It is always a shame to shut out that possibility altogether.

SUMMARY

- Show respect to your children by not submitting them to scenes that might shock or upset them.
- Tune in to your children's characters and try to be accordingly tactful.
- If in doubt, play down the relationship. This may avoid upsetting your children and if your man is worth knowing then he will understand.
- Remember that it's healthy to have a loving sexual relationship.

(11)

LEARNING TO LIVE IN A NEW FAMILY

'We need to move on from seeing the children of divorced and separated parents as having an experience which is essentially different from that of other children. All children experience a number of transitions that can be difficult for them, and for which they may require additional support.'

Joseph Rowntree Foundation, 2004

These are wise words and, although they ignore the fact that children of divorce do have an extra psychological task in learning to accept the two parents as separate individuals (see Chapter 8), the principle is an interesting one. We need to stop seeing separation and divorce as something radically different and instead accept that it is now standard behaviour for a very substantial minority – as many as one in three marriages. It is particularly important because most divorcing parents remarry relatively soon after divorce. The original family may have been broken up but a new family will have re-formed.

Bear in mind that the same Joseph Rowntree report found that the new step-family can have some very important effects on children.

- Younger children found a lot of support from being in the new family.
- Older siblings found it harder to adapt.
- Older children seemed to appreciate step-parents more when they acted in a supportive and friendly way *rather than being involved in discipline and control*.

A NEW FAMILY STRUCTURE

Remarriage (or living together) alters the structure of a family. The fact that, overnight, they acquire a whole new set of relations forces children to see themselves differently. The eldest child may find that she is no longer the head of the siblings; the youngest child, used to being spoilt as the baby, may find to her dismay that a new 'baby' has appeared on the scene. The younger child, used to being the buddy and support of her eldest sister, may find herself pushed out in the cold while the elder sister concentrates her companionship on a new stepsister. And of course, there is a whole new array of step-cousins, aunts, even grandparents.

- If the children have lived alone with their single parent for some time, they may resent the 'intrusion' of a step-parent and will jealously try to come between the new partners. Feelings of helplessness will be reinforced by not having the natural parent to turn to.
- A final loss in some families is where the children discover they are expected to forget about the natural parent and accept the new parent as a substitute. The Wallerstein and Kelly studies in the USA demonstrate this type of distress to such a painful degree that the researchers went on to stress the importance of

continuing access to the departed parent *as an aid to the children's acceptance of remarriage and a step-parent*.

- Relating to two fathers or two mothers poses some tricky questions too. Can I love two fathers? If I love one of them, will it mean the other feels rejected? Worse still, if I love one of them will the other reject me?

GAINS

However, all is not doom and gloom. Although the transition stage is potentially difficult, we should remind ourselves again that Mavis Hetherington's 2002 study showed 75 per cent of children doing well two years after the separation. It is with the aim of giving the remaining 25 per cent a better outcome and in particular, of improving life for the new step-family, that the following general principles for step-families are outlined.

- Remarriage often provides stability and a feeling of caring that the children have been forced to live without during the years of separation.
- The new relationship may provide a better model of caring and loving than has been available before.
- If the natural parent has previously suffered from depression, the arrival of the new spouse will probably remove the bad feelings and lighten the entire household.
- Without detracting from the qualities of the departed parent, the step-parent may fit well into the children's lives, may be more knowledgeable about their special interests, may provide a new dimension. Some people are naturally better parents than others. It could be that a step-parent is an improvement over the natural parent. But this doesn't have to pose a threat to the natural parent; there is room for both!

We know it is possible to enjoy a good family life in a remarriage; we know it is possible to continue a happy and loving relationship with the parent with access; we are becoming aware that flexible access to both families is best for the children concerned.

MANAGING THE MOVE TO THE STEP-FAMILY

- Introduce the new step-parent gradually, giving him/her a chance to *make friends* with the children.
- Make it clear that the inclusion of the step-parent does not mean the exclusion of the children.
- Continue to play an active part in the children's lives and do not dump them in the step-parent's lap.
- Allow the step-parent to acknowledge that he/she is *not* their natural parent and therefore cannot feel the same kind of love.
- Let the children know you believe the absent parent is still important to them and allow them as much access as is desired and as is possible.
- Talk about discipline in advance with your new partner. Make sure you both pursue exactly the same directions. Bear in mind the new finding that *step-relationships form better when the step-parent is not a heavy disciplinarian.*
- Compare notes continually with your new partner *and* with your ex-partner.
- Spend time with your step-children in order to help them with practical matters.

PROBLEMS

There are many practical difficulties that arise when any person has parental responsibility, but if you are an inexperienced step-mum or dad then some of the dilemmas you meet may be baffling. This next section tries to anticipate some of the most common problems that regularly arise in a new extended family.

Q I cannot like my two stepchildren. I feel extremely guilty about this and fall over backwards to be nice to them. But they really are little brats. I've been married to their father for six months now.

A Six months is too short a time in which to expect stepchildren to adjust totally to a new parent. Behave kindly but firmly to them. Don't overdo your patience, however. After six months it is time they began to modify their behaviour and think of your feelings as well as their own. Make it clear that you are a human being too and as such deserve some consideration. It may take between six months and three years for their feelings about you to settle down. If you can understand that they have probably had a lot of unpleasant changes to put up with, this might help you see things from their point of view. They need to learn to trust and rely on you.

What might these problems be? The children may feel that their mother has dumped them on you. Or they may resent you for (as they see it) usurping their mother's role.

There is no rule that says you *have* to like your stepchildren, though obviously it makes caring for them easier if you do. If you are able to satisfy your conscience that you are giving them the best attention they could get from you, then you are doing a good job.

Bear in mind that your behaviour now is setting a pattern for the future. So don't give in on battles you consider to be important because you feel guilty. If you do they will expect that in the future you will carry on giving in. Take a look at Chapter 12 for useful and constructive methods of working with children.

Try to assess how much anxiety your stepchildren are still genuinely feeling and how much they are simply playing you for a 'softie'. Above all, forget about feeling guilty. The majority of step-parents *don't* love their stepchildren as their own. That doesn't mean to say they can't get extremely fond of them over the years.

Q I am anxious to make a good relationship with my young stepson. His mother and I have been married for three years, and Harry is now aged eight. To begin with I didn't see much of him because he spent a lot of time with his father. Now he's at home with us more often. But I find my wife is overprotective. She's seen him hurt by his father and is terrified I will do the same. The result is that he looks on me with distrust because his mother has unwittingly taught him to do so.

A Your wife's feelings of concern are understandable. But you should also be able to feel you get a fair deal in your own home and should tackle your wife along these lines. There could be certain agreed rules about childcare, which the two of you could work out in advance. These ought to include specific activities that would allow you and your stepson to build up trust together. Help with homework, shared outings, games of football, things that feel friendly rather than fatherly.

You will need to reassure your wife, though, that you will avoid being critical of Harry, or negative to him, that you will give him encouragement (see page 124 in Chapter 12) and that you will keep your word, e.g. that any dates you make with the boy will be kept and that you will be generally trustworthy.

Household jobs where the two of you help each other would be a good way to connect. He would begin to see you as a workmate and as someone who allows him to feel free and feel good. Painting a garden wall is one messy but highly rewarding project. Helping with household carpentry and giving him his own set of tools is another. If you can cook, cake-making, rolling pastry and shape-cutting are perfect for shaping a better relationship. This all builds up the child's sense of security.

Q I am concerned that my husband constantly favours his children, often to the exclusion of mine. (We each have two daughters.) If tackled about it, he denies his behaviour and accuses me of being oversensitive. The trouble is, he honestly doesn't realise he's doing it. The result is that I find myself doing the same with my two, simply because I'm trying to compensate them for his behaviour. I'm sure this will be harmful for the children, probably giving rise to feelings of insecurity. How can I change things?

A Any child-minder who cares for extra children alongside her own will tell you that it is impossible to treat them equally. Subconsciously, most of us are tuned in to our children's special 'wavelengths' and it is not easy to pick up those of 'outsiders'. So a certain amount of favouritism is not only unavoidable, it's natural. And your own children should be able to accept this. Where such exclusion is harmful is if it is done spitefully or to excess. Assuming that this is not the case, you and your husband must just keep reminding yourselves to include each other's children. This way, the children won't get too much of a raw deal. I don't think it is a good idea, incidentally, to favour your children *in retaliation* for your husband's behaviour. Two wrongs don't make a right.

If your husband's exclusion of your children *is* done spitefully and if talking does not change his attitude, then you are put in the painful position of having to make a choice. There are three options. The first is that you do nothing and your children suffer. Second, that you think seriously about getting the children's natural father to have custody of them. Third, that you decide to set up a separate household from your second husband. None of these is pleasant but if your husband constantly subjects the children to unkindness, you are already in an unpleasant situation. Unpleasant situations call for unpleasant remedies.

However, there is the possibility that your husband's behaviour is a reflection of some unresolved problem he feels he has with you. If this *is* a possibility, you need to talk in depth with him to try and work out a solution. Going to a marriage guidance counsellor may be useful and should probably be done as soon as possible.

Q I have two sons and my second husband has one. My youngest son, who is used to being my baby, has now had his nose thoroughly put out of joint by the arrival of his stepbrother who is four years younger. Overnight he has become a 'middle child' and he doesn't like it. He seems to have regressed. He's been going to the toilet by himself for two years now, yet all of a sudden he appears unable to cope with cleaning himself and has to have me there to do it. I can understand why he's behaving like this but am finding it hard to cope, because inevitably I have my hands full looking after the demanding three-year-old stepson.

A Your youngest is going through a difficult transition and, stressful though it is, he does need your sympathy. He feels displaced and since he may already have felt rejected by your first husband's departure, perhaps the new stepbrother is adding to those feelings of rejection. Play along with him for a while. If he wants you in the bathroom, make allowances for him and play the game. After all, if he too were a three-year-old you would *have* to be there for him. He'll get over it and will soon think of something better to do.

Perhaps in your preoccupation with the three-year-old you have not concentrated as much as you might have on your son's needs. One option would be to regularly spend some time solely with your son – quality time! If it is impossible to do this while the three-year-old is around, arrange with your new husband that he takes complete charge of the baby every evening for an hour. That hour could then be devoted to the seven-year-old.

If this doesn't sound as if it would work, arrange for a relative or friend to take the three-year-old out for regular afternoons in the week. This could then be the seven-year-old's 'special' time. If you can keep this up for some months, your little boy should feel more secure.

You can gradually wean him off the special times when he seems able to manage without them. If he becomes upset again, simply continue them for a little longer. Incidentally, don't leave out the eldest child. Because he behaves happily, this doesn't mean to say he can't feel excluded too.

Q My husband's parents visit us often and every time they come over, they bring little presents for my husband's children. They do not, however, bring anything for *my* kids. This would be all right if my children's own grand-parents did likewise, but *they* usually only give presents at Christmas and on birthdays. My children feel this is very unfair and have become jealous of their stepbrother and stepsister. Is it unreasonable of me to expect these

grandparents either to bring something for all of them or not to bring anything at all? I don't want to be mean or unrealistic.

A You are not being mean or unrealistic. The grandparents are probably unaware of the bad feelings they create with their gifts and may only need this pointed out to them to reach their own solution. If they want to give presents to their own grandchildren, of course that's understandable. But ask them if they could include your kids, even if only on a small scale – say, by bringing them tiny toy cars, or a set of pencils or felt-tip pens.

If they react badly to your (tactful) suggestion, you are justified in being polite but firm to them. Explain that you understand their desire to please their grandchildren but that those same children are now part of a larger family. The children's situation has changed, and therefore, so has the grandparents'. If this still does not raise the required response, make it clear that any presents they bring will be regarded as joint family property.

This may not seem satisfactory but *the situation is an unsatisfactory one*. The alternative is to have one set of children feeling left out and the other set being spoilt, plus a great deal of internal bad feeling which you as their guardian could do without. You could account for your decision (about sharing) to your stepchildren by explaining that different sets of people have different rules and that what is right for their grandparents' home is not right for yours. They may not like it, but they will be able to understand it. It is important that you have your husband's backing on this issue, because if there continues to be ill feeling you don't want split sides within the camp.

Q I am about to marry a divorcee with a little daughter. I know nothing about children, particularly little girls.

I don't dislike them but just don't have a clue about how to behave. The child is six. I've never been interested in children nor particularly wanted any of my own, although I can see I might change my views on that. Naturally, I want my new marriage to work out and I'm anxious in case I mess it up by being an unsatisfactory stepfather. How should I behave?

A Why not regard making a relationship with your future stepdaughter as you would any subject you were about to study. If you were going to start a new study course or a work project, you would keep a low profile to begin with and let those in the know do the teaching. But you would pay attention, picking up as much as you could about the project until you began to feel you had something to contribute.

Look on your fiancée as the instructor and project leader. Spend time with her and the child, getting to know the child's interests, likes and dislikes. Be polite to her but if you don't feel you have anything to say, let her mother make the conversation and take the decisions. Ask your fiancée about the girl, find out what her daily routine is. What kind of a school does she go to? What kind of clothes does she like to wear? What does she do after school? Where does your fiancée see you fitting into the day-to-day routine?

Every child is an individual. Whereas one child may love being taken to the zoo and will respond eagerly to discussions about wildlife, another will turn up their nose at anything so unsophisticated and will instead go away and listen to the latest music on their iPod. It is this sort of detail that your fiancée can fill in.

If your fiancée is expecting you to provide some sort of discipline in the home, explain that you are willing to do so when you have got to know her daughter but that it's early days now and you would feel out of line telling someone who is a stranger what to do. Tell her that you only want do what she feels appropriate, and ask her to explain what she thinks would be best.

Don't rush things. The child may feel as nervous as you do. If, after you have lived together for a while, you find some of her behaviour unacceptable (she's rude, she eats with her mouth open, she won't answer you when you ask her something in front of other people), consult her mother. Work out with her the best way of tackling the child.

She certainly shouldn't be allowed to get away with being rude, but there may be overriding circumstances. As you begin to feel comfortable in your new home set-up, you will feel more confident. When that happens you will feel capable of dealing with your stepdaughter's problems and of making friendly overtures successfully.

Q My young stepchildren come back after weekends spent with their father feeling unsettled and behaving rather badly. My wife is concerned about them and thinks she should cut down the time they spend visiting their father. He is very opposed to this and thinks that if any change is made, he should see them *more* often. I sympathise with her and care about the children, but . . . they are not mine and I need the regular break from them that I get at the weekends. To tell the truth, I think I'd go spare if I didn't have that little bit of regular time to be alone with my wife. Our marriage will definitely suffer if this isn't taken into account. I can see this puts her in a dilemma, but what alternative is there?

A It sounds as though this is a case for you, your wife and her ex-husband to get together to discuss the children. This may sound a preposterous suggestion, but other couples do it and pool their common experience of the children with satisfactory results. All three of you have a point of view that needs to be taken into consideration. Come to that, so have the children.

Your wife should examine her reasons for *not* wanting the children to see her ex-husband more often. Could it be she is afraid of losing them? Extra time with their father might after all be a very satisfactory solution. Better for the children, better for him and good for the two of you. This is where you come in as a support and a consolation. If you make your married life with her so satisfactory that she feels completely secure, she will be able to risk the children staying away longer.

What do the children want? Has anyone thought of finding out? The best person to do this would be someone who is *not* so emotionally involved with them. It just might be a suitable job for you, their step-dad. Children are loyal. They might give a natural parent the answer they know the parent wants to hear, regardless of whether or not it is the truth. But with you, they are more likely to say what they really feel.

A certain amount of readjustment on the part of the children as they switch from home to home is natural. But children can and do cope with this kind of change. One option is to try leaving things as they are for a while. As life becomes more routine and more reliable, both she and the children will settle down. Often when the children appear unsettled, it is really one of the parents who is unsettled and who is unwittingly passing on those feelings.

If there is genuine cause for concern (the parent with access is neglecting the children or being cruel to them), you must naturally be prepared to rescue the children. But if the unsettled feelings stem mainly from coping with the changeover from one household to another, then *the sooner your wife can feel calm about it, the sooner the children will adjust.*

One of the great difficulties a step-parent has to cope with is the fact that his/her spouse, although divorced from the previous partner, *is still very much related because of the children*. One of the ways of continuing that relationship after divorce is by persistent squabbling with the ex-spouse. This just might be one of those cases.

If it is, your wife needs some counselling so that she can talk through her feelings. You are not necessarily the person with whom she should do this, since you have a vested interest in steering her off the subject. Encourage her to consult a marriage guidance counsellor. She might feel a lot better for it. And so, indirectly, would the rest of the family.

Q My husband very much wants me to have a baby. He has no children of his own but I have two sons from a previous marriage. I would quite like another baby but it's not on my list of priorities. I can understand, however, just how important it is for him. My main hesitation is based on my concern for my two boys. How are they going to react to a little half-brother or sister? Is it going to be very disturbing for them and heap anxieties on top of the problems already arising from the divorce? Is a new baby a wise move?

A It is unlikely that your children would be so disturbed by the advent of a new baby brother or sister that they would be seriously harmed for the rest of their lives. They certainly might suffer the inconvenience of a tired mother and an irritating junior member of the family, but eventually the tiredness stops and the baby grows up.

Every child fears displacement by the birth of a new baby, and some displacement is inevitable. When you have a tiny helpless infant which needs constant attention, you simply cannot spend as much time and energy on the older children as they have been used to. But this is true of any family.

The real question is, will it exacerbate your children's insecurities? It is impossible to know because so much depends on what the divorce was like and how settled the children's background is now.

Provided you, the children and their stepfather have been living a settled life together for the past couple of years, and provided there is a minimum of conflict between yourself and their father, then the children will probably react to the baby much as they would to any new baby sibling.

If, on the other hand, your divorce was fraught with drama, the separation has been notable for the fights with your ex, and the children have been relentlessly used as weapons, then yes, they might be upset. They will have learned to distrust most of the moves made by their parents. *You are the only person who can ultimately decide on extending your family.*

Q My husband has (mutually agreed) custody of our two daughters, but they spend a great deal of time with me and my new husband; about two-thirds with my ex-husband and one-third with me. The problems arise from the relationship of my girls with my new partner. He is their stepfather but doesn't really feel like one because the girls don't actually live in our home. He has occasional contact with them and is therefore expected to share those occasional parts of their lives. Yet he has no real rights of control, which means he feels ineffective and superfluous. Naturally, he dislikes this and tends to opt out of their lives altogether, which distresses me as nothing would please me more than for us all to play happy families together.

A You can't force anyone to enjoy a relationship and the kind of part-time stepfather you have just described has a tricky role. Perhaps you should work out two things. The first is to make it clear to the children that there are rules and regulations in your home and they have to abide by these, just as they have to abide by their father's rules in his house. It would be helpful if there were similar standards in both your children's homes and discussing these with your ex might be very constructive. Children need boundaries and if they know what to expect from their routine, even if it differs between homes, they will feel more secure in themselves.

Although you can tactfully keep trying to involve your new partner in your family life, if he continues to be reluctant, you must accept that he and the children will have to spend a lot of time apart. This may hurt you, and may disillusion you about his family sensibilities. But you will have to incorporate his lack of involvement into your lifestyle.

This is not an excuse for bad behaviour on his part, of course. Certainly you and the children have every right to expect him to be polite and kind on the occasions they meet. But you would be sensible to plan your activities with the children without taking it for granted he will want to be included. Over the months, *he will grow more used to your girls*. He may even join in eventually. But he needs time to get used to family life. Meanwhile, you have got to think of their life with you and make that satisfactory.

As the parent with access, you are probably trying to recreate the kind of family life you had together before the divorce. But you will need to come to terms with the fact that the old family no longer exists, and therefore *the old family lifestyle cannot either*. Enjoy the children's company for their own sake.

Q My three stepchildren see me as responsible for the break-up of their mother's marriage. They are right to think this but ignore the circumstances which led to their mother wanting a new relationship in the first place. (She found their father a very unsatisfactory husband.) They choose to think of me as an unfortunate fad in their mother's life and not worth serious attention. It's extremely annoying for me when, in front of others, I say something to one of them and find myself ignored. They pursue this to the point of rudeness and I can't see any likelihood of change. Their mother is extremely upset by it but has been unable to change them. The oldest boy is eighteen, shortly to go to university, the other boy is sixteen and already out at work, while the girl is thirteen and still at school.

A Unfortunately, older children do tend to find adjusting to a new step-parent difficult. It sounds as if they were extremely distressed by their parents' divorce and are coping with the pain by blocking out the person they see as responsible. It probably wouldn't help to tell them their father was partly responsible for the divorce as that would hurt even more.

If they can't alter their behaviour there are two things you could do. You can put up with the situation but *insist* on politeness from them. Talk to them about this, making it clear that (a) you are entitled to politeness and (b) they are showing themselves up badly by such rudeness.

You could also console yourself with the fact that the eldest will virtually have left home once he goes to university. Once he has gone, the middle child may calm down without his influence. If he doesn't, you could encourage him to find his own place to live.

The best way to do this is to give him two options. You can tell him that you are very happy he should continue living with you provided he behaves politely. If he is not able to do that, then he should find his own accommodation. You can offer to help him do so and also to make the move. It could be made clear that you and his mother will always be there to support him in times of trouble. In this way you will be setting him a reasonable boundary.

This leaves the thirteen-year-old daughter. Away from her brothers' antagonism, it is very likely that her feelings will change. As she is younger, she may have a more open mind, with fewer preconceived ideas about you. If the worst comes to the worst, at least there would only be one child left in the camp instead of three.

I appreciate you may not want to be seen as the person who is physically displacing the children. Obviously you must gauge just how uncomfortable home circumstances are before making these moves. But you are entitled to a certain consideration in your own home and if your nearly adult stepchildren are unwilling to grant it, they must accept the logical consequences.

PERSONAL ADVICE

Phillip Hodson is a marriage counsellor, fellow of the British Association for Counselling and Psychotherapy and part-time stepfather to my eldest children. He sees step-parenthood as offering both joys and concerns.

The cons
'When you acquire a ready-made family,' he says, 'you acquire young people with values and standards quite different from your own. There may be a culture clash between you; there may be a

class difference. Your ideas of children's obedience may not be theirs. Their physical rhythms may differ from yours.

'If you come from a boisterous family you may not like a shy child and vice versa. You may be jealous of the children or they may be jealous of you. When the chips are down, who will your partner choose? You or them? It's uncomfortable to think it might not be you.

'You have no natural commitment to the child, only indirect acquired commitment. You don't have the natural parent's instinct for doing things for the children without thinking twice and you may not understand what the children expect from you. If stepchildren trade on you – over money, say – you feel resentful. Because there is no natural bond, their needs for money can seem a drain, whereas if it were your own flesh and blood you probably wouldn't think twice about it.

'No matter what a step-parent may say, it's the spouse you chose to marry, not the children. I think it's vital that the natural parent, and indeed the step-parent too, understands that it is natural *not* to possess the instinctive concern for children that a real parent has.'

The pros

'On the other hand, you acquire a ready-made family with none of the hard work involved. You haven't had the exhausting nights, the years of discipline, the childhood diseases to cope with. If you are lucky you may find you now have perfectly charming children who are a pleasure to be with and who adapt easily and readily to their new family life with you. You are wanted and needed by the children as well as by the new partner which, if caring is what you are seeking, may be extremely pleasant. If the children are similar in character to their natural parent whom you love and have chosen to live with, you may find them a double bonus.

'Step-parents won't feel the same about the children year in, year out. They will pass through a number of phases. They may like the kids initially, then find the reality of living together quite different. Eventually, over the years, you and the kids mellow and improve. One day you realise, with pleasure, that you like them quite a lot.'

How might a step-parent overcome the difficulties?

'Accept reality,' Phillip says, 'don't try to treat the children as if they are your own. Get along with them as well as you can. It helps to establish house rules and to stick to your promises. Try to cultivate the positive sides of their characters that appeal to you: establish common ground, over mutual interests and hobbies. Encourage their achievements but do *not* criticise their failures.

'It's important to realise that they are separate human beings and entitled to a certain amount of space, just as you are. Don't be a martyr, though. Don't go tearing off to a rock concert you hate, or a film you know you will loathe, just because they want you to. They will learn to take advantage of you and ultimately will lose respect for you. But keep a watch for movies you *both* want to see, so that you are not continually turning down their approaches.'

Respect your stepchildren

'I must stress that *you have to respect the children as individuals*. They should be given their own space and rights. It's vital to agree with their natural parent *right from the start* what your role is going to be. There is nothing more undermining than taking a firm line with the children only to find that your spouse is busy refuting your words of wisdom.

'If you can manage to follow this advice, you should be able to feel confident that whatever their eventual reaction is to you, you have done the right thing by them. With any luck, you'll end up enjoying a very happy family life.' And do not forget that they as individuals may have much to teach you, that your own life can be enriched by their very difference.

SUMMARY

- Introduce a step-parent-to-be gradually.
- Do not expect the children to automatically like him/her.
- Do not expect him/her to automatically like the children.
- Establish a few boundaries and house rules to help the children know what to do and what not to do. But don't hedge them in.
- If a child behaves badly, give him/her options to choose from. But explain that there are consequences to choices.

HELPFUL CHILD-REARING METHODS

All parents meet with difficulties when raising their children. The children's misbehaviour, regardless of divorce or separation, depends on the behaviour patterns they have *always* followed in your home. In this chapter I outline some of these patterns and describe some very specific child-rearing methods that take them into account. These methods help children cope with *many* difficult situations in life – not only those connected with divorce. However, as explained in the previous chapter, some children will act up after their parents' separation. Being able to fall back on some tried and true child-management skills can be extremely helpful.

These skills are based on the educational ideas of founding psychologist Alfred Adler. A contemporary of Freud and Jung, Adler was much more down to earth than his colleagues and considered that children, from the very beginning, strive to 'carve out' their place in the world and hence develop their own self-worth. Since to small children the world is the immediate family, *the children begin the process by trying to find their place within the family.*

This is a useful concept, not least because it means that parents have some control over that world, even if they have divorced.

THE KEY TO HAPPY CHILDREN

The key aspects to child-rearing therefore, according to Adler and his great disciple Rudolf Dreikurs (who broadly expanded the ideas into working methods for parents to use with children), are:

- plenty of encouragement
- understanding the meaning behind children's misbehaviour
- helping the children find their place in the family, which involves understanding how birth order affects children's behaviour
- teaching the children to co-operate
- teaching the children to take responsibility and to learn the consequences of their behaviour.

Simple parental goals, but just how do you put them into action?

ENCOURAGEMENT

I used to think that encouragement meant praise. The Adlerians, however, consider that praise isn't quite right. If you say, 'What a good boy,' when Johnny has brushed his teeth without being reminded, the problem is that Johnny might also get the idea in his head that if he *doesn't* brush his teeth he is bad and therefore unlovable.

If, on the other hand, you say, 'I particularly like the way you brushed at the back of your mouth,' you are commenting favourably *on a skill* that Johnny has developed and he will grow in self-esteem. That is encouragement.

What you should *not* do is comment negatively and criticise. Always try to find something of value in your children's behaviour even if you don't like what they are doing. This can be tough when he/she is being a complete monster; nevertheless children respond to encouragement far better than they do to criticism.

Children are emotionally damaged by continual criticism and respond in one of two ways. The first is that they become extremely depressed and don't function very well in the world at all. The second is that they become extremely angry and do their best to make life impossible for the person they feel angry with. It makes sense to try to avoid this.

Respect is a key word in this philosophy. Children learn respect from seeing it demonstrated. This doesn't mean that children have the same life experience or knowledge as you do. Of course they don't. But both you and your children are human beings and as such you both deserve respect. This doesn't mean:

- that your children may blithely ignore you
- that they may tell you what to do
- or that they are in charge rather than you.

It is your job to teach and train your children. But this needs to be done respectfully. So if your difficult child actually does something you've asked him/her to do, thank him/her for doing it. You will quite soon see a better-behaved youngster.

MISBEHAVIOUR

Adler's theory is that *each and every* behaviour has a purpose. With children, four types of misbehaviour are considered particularly important. These are:

- attention seeking
- power/control
- revenge
- withdrawal.

When *you* as a parent experience these, the emotions you are likely to feel in response are:

- irritation
- anger
- hurt
- despair.

In fact you can actually identify exactly what your children's behaviour is from the feelings that *you* experience. When Johnny whines about his little brother yet again, the fact that you feel extreme irritation has meaning. This is seriously useful because it is the beginning of seeing your way into managing Johnny's problem.

Adler believes that 'emotions are actually a form of thinking,' that 'people control their emotions through controlling their thinking'. For example:

Attention seeking

Jessica winds herself around her father's legs every time a friend comes round to chat, forcing the attention to be focused on her, rather than father or friend. Her father feels *irritated*.

Power/control

Sam has recently taken to having a tantrum at the checkout counter when his mother refuses to buy him sweets. He won't listen to reason, won't respond to her requests or orders and makes it almost impossible to deal with the shopping at the till. His mother feels *angry*.

Revenge

Annie tells her mother that the nice dessert her mother has spent a lot of time preparing for the family is disgusting. Her mother feels *hurt*.

Withdrawal

Max has got so far behind in coping with his maths homework that he gives up now almost as soon as he starts on it. His father, who is trying to help him, feels *despairing*.

The parents' usual reaction to:

- *irritation* is to snap and push the person away
- *anger* is to fight back in a battle for control
- *hurt* is to hurt back or to retreat wounded
- *despair* is to give up just as the other person has already done.

The great strength of being able to 'read' the emotion behind the child's misbehaviour is that it gives useful information about *how bad the child may be feeling*.

   Each of these misbehaviours is related to degrees of insecurity and discouragement. They show that your children are feeling discouraged. *Attention-seekers are the least discouraged children* and the *withdrawn the most discouraged*. The other two behaviours fall somewhere in the middle. The solutions are not to snap back or to punish but to look instead at the degree of upset your children are experiencing and then set about trying to reduce it. If you can reduce their distress (however well disguised it may be), you can change their behaviour for the better. This might be done simply through your encouragement. Or the children might need some specific teaching or simple strategies. I put forward some of these later in this chapter.

HELPING THE CHILDREN FIND THEIR PLACE IN THE FAMILY

Have you ever wondered why three children from the same family with an absolutely identical upbringing might turn out so differently? The answer is that being born into different birth positions within the family automatically sets them up to have a different experience of that family. Each child is striving for recognition and a sense of value within the family, *but from different perspectives*.

First Born
First Borns receive a great deal of parental attention, partly because they are the first, partly because there is no one else to compete for attention. This means that when the second child is born, First Borns find it hard to relinquish the attention. As a result they may become bossy and angry. But, on the plus side, First Borns most often make excellent leaders and often learn to be responsible from an early age.

Second Born
Try as they may, Second Borns can never catch up with First Borns however hard they work. But the habit of hard work may stand them in good stead when older because they will be 'sloggers' who achieve their aims. They also desperately want to be different from the first. This means that they may make a point of behaving quite differently. For example, if the First Born is dreamy then the Second Born will be practical.

The Middle Child

If a third child is born, the second one becomes a 'Middle'. Middle children are by definition 'squeezed'. They can never quite catch up with the first, but they have already been superseded, as far as their parents' attention is concerned, by the third. Some Middle children react by becoming unhappy, 'spikey' individuals. Others learn ways to get along with everyone and become very adept at keeping and maintaining friendships.

Youngest Born

These are always the babies of the family. Someone has trodden the difficult paths of 'growing up' before them. As a result life tends to be easier. Things get done for them since there are older family members to help. They are often incredibly charming. Some Youngest Born work incredibly hard to keep up with the others, but a few give up because they feel they will never catch up.

The Only Child

Often called the 'spoilt' only child, these are used to having everyone's attention without needing to compete. They may not find it so easy to get on with contemporaries because they haven't had to do this in the family. They can be self-assured, sometimes pushy, and often creative.

The Family Constellation

Now you can see just how differently life can turn out for each family member. But there's another aspect to family dynamics. It's that of the Family Constellation. It helps to think about *all* the many ways in which we may be affected by family.

To get a full idea of your own Family Constellation, these are the questions you need to ask yourself.

- How many brothers and sisters do you have?
- Where does your birth order lie in this family?
- Were there any stillbirths, miscarriages or the early death of a child? This may turn out to be important because if your mother had a baby before you that died, your birth may be desperately important to her, conferring special status, or resented, since she may feel that nobody could ever replace the dead child.
- Were there other household members such as grandparents, aunts, uncles, near neighbours who you were particularly close to? These are important too because the views, life experience and humour of these close others will also influence how you grew up understanding the world.

And just as these factors affected *you*, they will also be influencing your own children.

How does any of this relate to divorce or separation? It helps you understand why children in your family react differently to the same unhappy circumstances. It also helps by allowing you to treat each child differently, since you will now be able to see that each comes from a subtly individual perspective, with subtly different influences from the people they felt close to. Because of this, each will cope with divorce accordingly.

SUMMARY SO FAR

- Children (unconsciously) use attention seeking, power/control, revenge or withdrawal in mistaken attempts to make themselves valuable and to find their place in the family.
- Children are easily discouraged, which is why they revert to these behaviours. It's therefore important that we give them constant encouragement.

- It is vital to show that you respect both your children and others. This means refraining from criticism as well as positively acknowledging helpful behaviour.
- Birth Order and Family Constellation can offer clues to a child's individual view of the world.

TEACHING THE CHILDREN TO CO-OPERATE

Getting children to work together is not easy, since they haven't yet learned to think of others. And yet this is sometimes very necessary, especially when you are experiencing pain and grief at the end of a marriage or relationship. There are specific methods that help children understand the idea of how working together can be rewarding. One of these is the notion of the Family Meeting.

The Family Meeting

- Anyone in the family can call a family meeting. He or she sets a specific time for it and when you are all seated around the kitchen table, he or she hands out an Agenda. Even quite young children can do this, with a little help from their elders.
- The Agenda can include any kind of issue, from sorting out who watches which television programme, to very specific and problematic issues such as 'I don't want to go to Dad's this weekend'. You can stick the Agenda on the family noticeboard or the fridge door in advance so that others can add to it if they want.
- One person will need to be in charge of the meeting, and to begin with it will need to be a grown-up. But once the children have got the idea of how it works, then they can take turns at being in charge too.

- One person will need to take notes of the meeting, which can also be stuck on the noticeboard or fridge later on so that everyone can read them and remember the decisions. Once again this may need to be done by a grown-up to begin with, but it can fairly easily be done by a child once they understand the proceedings.

Family Meeting issues

- As each issue is read it will need to be discussed.
- Letting the children discuss first allows them to feel important.
- If anyone is shy about coming forward, encourage them to do so, asking for their opinion.
- Limit complaints, otherwise the sessions turn into a series of depressing gripes.
- You can move on the conversation by asking, 'What can we do about this problem? What ideas/solutions do people have?' And then listen to them carefully.
- If there are a number of family jobs that need to be done (such as making beds, emptying rubbish or the dishwasher), ask people to write these on slips of paper and put them in a jobs pile in the middle of the table. Once they are all decided on, ask for volunteers. If you don't get any volunteers, then inform the family that the decisions will be made by each person drawing out a slip of paper until all the slips have gone.
- It needs to be made clear that once agreement has been reached in the Family Meeting about who is doing which job, the jobs have to be carried out before the next meeting. If the children want to swap jobs after the meeting, that is up to them, but the jobs must be done.

Trouble shooting

- What happens if the jobs don't get done? Apologies certainly help if this happens. But if it goes on happening, then a rule needs to be agreed that before people do pleasurable activities their chores must be carried out first. This applies to parents as well as children, and all family members are considered equal here. It is amazing how a joint consensus, from everyone in the family, makes individual members want to do their part.

- To avoid Family Meetings becoming merely gripe sessions, it's important to table 'good' points for discussion. You might start by sharing good things that have happened in the previous week. You may congratulate someone on a job well done. You can thank people for help. And after the meeting you might plan some little fun enterprise – a game, a story, even a large chocolate cake!

- In case this sounds as if it's very adult-led, it can be remarkable how quickly the children get used to the idea and, following your example, start running the meetings themselves.

- Family Meetings can include any important family member. This might be the parent who now lives away, a step-parent, stepbrothers/sisters and even grandparents. At the meeting everyone's view is listened to, respected and dealt with, as if in a business meeting. If someone shows disrespect instead of getting angry, just say, 'I'm worried that name-calling might stop us co-operating. Let's concentrate on the issues instead.'

TEACHING THE CHILDREN TO TAKE RESPONSIBILITY – TRAINING

It becomes especially important after a family splits up that you can all rely on each other. You need each other in a way that perhaps other families do not. Yet we *all* have to learn responsibility and in these days where children tend to be over-protected, this isn't always straightforward. The first thing you might usefully do is set the children a good example. Consciously or unconsciously, children learn behaviour from those they are closest to. Even if, later on, they choose to behave differently, nevertheless those good examples will be instilled inside them.

So what are the best ways of doing this? You might:

- bite back angry words and look for positive ways of arguing
- set to with a will in order to complete a task
- cuddle family members at every available opportunity
- keep the home tidy and (to begin with) help the children keep their rooms tidy.

There are some very specific skills that come in useful here. One example is really listening to what your children are trying to explain instead of thinking about the relative calm of the office.

Listening skills

These are as simple as really tuning in to what the children are saying instead of just letting it glide over you. Part of being respectful (and coincidentally teaching your children respect) is to take someone seriously. Listening isn't only about listening, however – there are also follow-ups that extend listening. Really good listening entails the following steps:

1. **Listen to what they say.**
2. **'Hear' what is being said.** This means looking out for other signs, such as body language, that will tell you what your children are really feeling. They may be scowling, pulling faces, or wriggling. Don't assume anything.

3. **Think of yourself as a mirror.** If you can see a particular feeling that your children are showing, reflect it back: 'I can see that this is really difficult for you to talk about.' 'Your face makes you look very unhappy.' 'I can see that you are trying to hide, so I guess you are feeling worried or guilty about something. I promise you that I won't get angry about it. So why don't you tell me what's going on?' (*Having promised that you won't get angry, now you have to keep your promise. However, if something pretty dreadful has happened, that doesn't mean that you can't sort out ways in which your children can work towards improving things again.*)

4. When you have drawn out your children as far as you believe possible, **start working on non-punishing solutions**. These need to be tasks that they can realistically carry out.

5. **Thank the children respectfully** for the assistance they have given you, when eventually the tasks are completed.

Listening to what your children are feeling and saying is just the first part of working towards *them* taking responsibility for *their* lives. In order to learn what will happen if they *don't* take responsibility for themselves, they need to learn the consequences of their behaviour.

Consequences and options

Among the useful concepts offered is the one of **natural and logical consequences**.

- A **natural consequence** might occur when a child goes to school without her raincoat and gets wet.
- A **logical consequence** arrives when the child is told that she has a choice in what happens next. For example, Dad might tell his daughter that it looks like rain and therefore she needs to

remember to take her raincoat. He might remind her a couple of times but not more. If in the end she can't be bothered to remember, partly because she's relying on Dad too much, she will of course get wet should it rain.

By offering her choices you are also letting her see that she genuinely possesses **options** and therefore some control over her life. Getting wet in this instance is *what she opted for*. She has controlled the situation even if it ended uncomfortably. This can be surprisingly educational. *Of course the consequences need to be structured. No parent can allow a consequence that will be physically harmful or dangerous.*

Coming from 'I'

This is a discipline that applies as well to grown-ups as it does to children.

The trouble with saying 'You did this' and 'You did that' is that it sounds accusatory. If you want someone to actually listen to what you say without immediately feeling forced to go into self-defence mode and therefore tune out from your concern, it is much more sensible to say 'I'.

'I feel very let down when the dishwasher is never unloaded. I feel as if everyone expects me to do all the work.'

Practise doing this in your head a few times before applying it to family problems.

Whose problem is it?

This is a good question and one that often applies to the perennial difficulty of children who never clear up their room. You may nag children about not doing the clearing up but if you ask yourself who does this matter to, the answer invariably comes back that it is *your* problem and not the children's. That is because the children invariably feel perfectly happy in their mess.

You may want to compromise and tell your *younger* child that you will help it make a start on clearing up. If your *older* child refuses to comply, you might then use Logical Consequences on it:

'It is your choice to live in a mess but it is my choice to occasionally clear up. This means that all your rubbish will be put into black plastic sacks and ranged along the wall. If you don't like this because you now can't find something, then I will remind you that you had the choice of clearing up yourself and you declined.'

Your own anger

You need to be careful when you are angry. Remind yourself that if you are going to get engaged in a struggle, some of the techniques outlined in this chapter will help the situation. Focus on finding ways through the difficulty rather than exploding. And if you feel you are becoming uncontrollably angry, walk away. Literally walk out of the room until you have cooled off.

Brainstorming

This is something that regularly happens at a Family Meeting but sometimes it's an activity that can be carried out by only two of you. It just takes sitting down with a pad and paper and writing down every solution that comes to mind. Another method is to give each child strips of paper and get them to write down an idea on each strip and then throw it into a pile. At the end of the session, someone can read through all the strips (ideas). And then everyone can discuss them. Do not rubbish other people's ideas. Respectfully detail why the ideas may work and why they may not.

And explain to the children that this is how you *all* approach brainstorming. The children need to learn to generate and react to ideas in the same way.

Take time for training

The methods I've just outlined often need individual explanation. This takes time. It can also take time for an idea to be understood, so be prepared for this. Timetable your day so that there are distinct periods when you can get together with the children to go over training methods.

Training also involves teaching your children the basic skills they will need to get by in life, such as dressing themselves and getting ready for school.

Make simple requests

If you clutter your children's minds up with too much detail or too many requests at the same time, they get confused and don't know where to start.

- Keep it simple.
- Deal with one thing at a time.

Avoid pity

This is hard for a loving parent to accept, but it is important that your children learn to deal with disappointment. There will, sadly, be a great deal of this in their adult life and knowing that you can slog through it and get out the other side is a great asset. So:

- Don't show pity.
- Don't try and make up for a disappointment.
- But do sympathise.

- Do be supportive.
- Do help them come up with alternative possibilities.

Disappointment can drain away hope. Finding hope in something else can be wonderful.

Have fun together often

Getting out and doing something completely different can be a great healer. When your mind is taken off something sad, you feel better when you return to contemplating the sad event. And even if you are living in the most difficult circumstances and coping with the aftermath of separation, it's possible to find activities that make you smile. You might:

- Go to the park and meet with other families.
- Join an organisation like your local branch of Gingerbread and enjoy their social activities and make new friends.
- Arrange tiny surprises or rewards and dole them out when least expected.
- Go on camping holidays.
- Make a hedgehog cake.
- Dress up in fancy dress and open the front door to the children after school as a surprise.
- Tell your children often how much you appreciate the help and support they give you.

SUMMARY SO FAR

- Use the Family Meeting method to teach the children to pull together and start taking responsibility.
- Really listen to your children and watch out for their body language as well as their words!

- Don't cosset the children. Let them find out the consequences of their own actions (within reason!).
- Don't criticise by saying 'you'. Always come from 'I'. That allows the children to see you as a person affected by their behaviour and prevents them from instantly blocking off your comments.
- Work out who is really affected by something. Is it the children? Or is it you?
- Control your anger.
- Make time for training your children in these methods even if it's difficult to do so.
- Keep it simple.
- Don't show pity.
- Have as much fun as possible!

THE MOST COMMON FAMILY PROBLEMS

Tantrums

Use Consequences and Options. 'If you continue to behave like this you are going to have to stay in your room until you feel like behaving better. When you are prepared to do this, then you can come back.'

Or 'You have a choice. You can either come with me to the supermarket and behave well. Or, if you are going to behave badly at the checkout counter, then you can stay at Auntie Betty's instead and I will pick you up when I come back.'

And you *must* carry out what you have outlined. If you go back on your words your children will never take you seriously.

Room tidying

Use Family Meeting and Consequences. See pages 131 and 135.

Getting dressed in the morning

Use Encouragement and *Training,* see pages 124 and 133. All children should be able to dress themselves by the time they are four. Some educators specify earlier. Children need to be taught how to do this and will need help to begin with. But do not fall into the trap of *always* helping. Even if they don't get it quite right, congratulate them on their speed, deftness and quick learning. You could make a start each evening by putting out their clothes for the following day. And you could go on to teach them that if they choose their own clothes the night before, they can wear their favourites.

Getting ready for school on time

Use Family Meeting, Training and *Consequences,* pages 131, 133 and 135. This can be a problem with older children. However, many parents take part in a communal school run and your younger children may need to be ready for collection. Or they may travel on a school bus. This means they need to be dressed, washed and breakfasted by a certain time with their school things packed.

This is an example of a situation where putting in a bit of time on training the children pays off. Work with the children on learning to get ready the night before. Suggest that they put out the clothes they will need in the morning on a chair. Advise them to make their packed lunch the night before and provide containers and airtight wrapping. Teach them to use an alarm clock. If they persistently fail to be ready on time, use *Options* (page 135) to let them know that they will be put on the bus regardless of how they are dressed, with or without their school things.

You must of course carry this through if the children challenge you. Ensure that they understand clearly that they have it within their power to avoid this shaming experience and that going through such a situation is entirely their own choice. The alternative lies within their hands. Don't do this in any way vengefully.

Simply carry through with the explanations just as you would any other choices they want to make. Remind them that if they are upset, they can call a Family Meeting to sort things out further.

Doing household chores such as tidying the room
See *Whose Problem is It?* (page 136).

Continually beating up a brother or sister
Use Encouragement (page 124) and *Listening Skills* (page 134). Children are aggressive because they feel bad about themselves. Find out what is going on that makes them feel so unhappy. If they don't want to talk, try bouncing a few of your own ideas off them:

> *'I have a feeling that you are angry about Dad living on the other side of town.'*

They may deny it or shrug it off but their body language may disclose something else. There's a tell-tale wriggle that small children make when they are telling untruths. You can see them contemplating your words. Watch out for small signs of recognition. If you think you have gained some idea of their distress, ask them what they think might make things better. Tell them how much you appreciate some aspect of their behaviour that is admirable. Tell them how much you value their love and support.

If the child needs some time for him/herself, try to make the time, however difficult. If it's impossible, arrange for a close family member to give them the time they need. I shall forever be grateful to *my* uncle for seeing me as an interesting human being with whom he chose to spend time. Other people can and do help.

EXTRA READING

Of course there are many other familiar family problems. The methods briefly outlined in this chapter can and will help. If you would like to know more, there are two marvellous books on the subject. One is *The Parent's Handbook* by Don Dinkmeyer Sr, Gary D. MacKay and Don Dinkmeyer Jr, published by Random House and the other is *Happy Children* by Rudolf Dreikurs and Vicki Soltz RN, published by Dutton Books.

EPILOGUE

I am an optimist. I do believe that, however painful and impossible your divorce or separation seems during its time of crisis, your lifestyle will eventually be sorted out and your grief diminish. When you look back, it will feel good to know that, however arrangements for the children ultimately turned out, you did your best for them at a time when your own life was at breaking point. We all have strengths and weaknesses. It may be far harder for some of us to cope with distress and grief than it is for others. But, regardless of pain thresholds, we can do our best to provide the happiest background possible for the children even in unhappy circumstances.

Yes, of course the children will be sad that their parents no longer live together. But they need not be permanently damaged if you and your ex-spouse or partner put them first and remember that they are human beings, not possessions.

Social change starts in a small way. Let's hope that with shifting attitudes to marriage and divorce, it is recognised that divorce or separation does not signify failure on the part of the participants. Rather, it shows growth and emotional development. People who divorce or split up are people reaching out for a different state of mind and a fresh stage to their life. What we need to learn is how to change in a responsible fashion. Responsibility, I believe, begins with the family.

APPENDIX 1 EMOTIONAL AND PRACTICAL SUPPORT

ORGANISATIONS

Child Poverty Action Group
94 White Lion Street, London N1 9PF. Tel: 020 7833 4627
Web: cpag.org.uk
Email: advice@cpag.org.uk

Offers advice and help for low-income families on welfare benefits and other matters.

Families Need Fathers
134 Curtain Road, London EC2A 3AR
Tel: 020 7613 5060
24 hour helpline: 020 8295 1956/01920 462825
Web: www.fnf.org.uk
Email: www.fnf.org.uk

A registered UK charity founded in 1974, which provides information and support to parents, including unmarried parents of either sex. FNF is chiefly concerned with the problems of maintaining a child's relationship with both parents during and after family breakdown.

Fathers Direct

Herald House, Lambs Passage, Bunhill Row, London EC1Y 8TQ
Tel: 0845 634 1328
Web: www.fathersdirect.com

The UK's national information centre for fatherhood. Fathers Direct is a charity founded in 1999 by professionals with expertise in social work, family policy, business development and communications.

Friends and Family of Lesbians and Gays (FFLAG)

7 York Court, Wilder Street, Bristol BS2 8HQ
Tel: 0117 942 9311
Helpline: 01454 852418
Web: www.fflag.org.uk

A national voluntary organisation set up in 1993 by parents of lesbian daughters and gay sons who work through confidential helplines and parents' groups. FFLAG helps and supports other parents and family members who have difficulty in understanding and accepting their child's sexuality.

Gingerbread

7 Sovereign Close, Sovereign Court, London E1W 2HW
Tel: 020 7488 9300
Fax: 020 7488 9333
Advice line and membership: Freephone 0800 018 4318
Web: www.gingerbread.org.uk
Email: office@gingerbread.org.uk

A nationally organised self-help association for one-parent families. Membership is open to anyone who shares its aims and objectives. At the time of writing, there are local groups in all parts of the country. The groups meet regularly and arrange social activities for parents and children, and practical help is given to members on a co-operative and collective basis. In Liverpool there is a 'pop-in' centre where a local solicitor offers help and advice.

Gingerbread supplies a number of leaflets on legal rights, housing, mortgages, and future income, plus advice to parents on a wide variety of problems. Help is given not only to members but to all lone parents.

Jewish help

There are a variety of organisations specialising in emotional and practical help for Jews. The *Jewish Year Book*, available from libraries, lists all social work help, family casework services, help for children, grants and accommodation.

Mothers Apart from their Children (MATCH)

BM Problems, London WC1N 3XX
Web: www.matchmothers.org

A group of divorced or separated mothers who have chosen to let their ex-husbands have custody of their children. MATCH provides a crisis counselling service, emotional support and a media service, which aims to inform the public that the decision to live apart from the children can be a responsible and caring one.

NCH – the children's charity
85 Highbury Park, London N5 1UD
Tel: 020 7704 7000
Web: www.nch.org.uk

As well as running many children's homes across the country, NCH gives help to families, including financial and housing aid. It employs full-time social workers, runs family centres incorporating twelve-hour day care with medical and educational facilities, and can help with accommodation often specially designed for one-parent families. It also runs advice centres and playgroups.

National Family Mediation
Alexander House, Telephone Avenue, Bristol BS1 4BS
Tel: 0117 904 2825
Fax: 0117 904 3331
Web: www.nfm.u-net.com
Email: general@nfm.org.uk

Provides a network of Family Mediation Services in England and Wales. Its web site lists mediation services in your area of the United Kingdom.

National Federation of Solo Clubs
8 Ruskin Chambers, 191 Corporation Street, Birmingham B4 6RY
Tel: 0121 236 2879

Tries to provide singles with a social life. It has 150 local branches, which regularly advertise in the classified columns of local newspapers. The branches organise meetings, dancing, theatre parties, coach trips, outings and so on for lonely men and women and their children. It has a benevolent fund and can provide holiday help. It also supplies a booklet entitled *Facing Life Alone*.

One Parent Families
255 Kentish Town Road, London NW5 2LX
Tel: 020 7428 5400
Fax: 020 7482 4851
Helpline (free and confidential): 0800 018 5026
Web: oneparentfamilies.org.uk

The only national charity which deals exclusively and professionally with *all* problems faced by one-parent families. It advises individuals, the public and the government on matters of family law, childcare, poverty, welfare rights, housing, health, tax, employment, and emotional problems.

One Parent Families Scotland
13 Grayfield Square, Edinburgh EH1 3NX
Helpline: 0800 018 5026
Web: opfs.org.uk
Email: info@opfs.org.uk

Offers advice, information and referral, and sorts out appropriate services for single-parent families. It holds conferences and has a list of useful publications available by mail order.

Professional Classes Aid Council
10 St Christopher's Place, London W1V 1HZ
Tel: 01452 331131
Web: www.pcac.org.uk
Email: admin@pcac.org.uk

Helps professionals, including single parents, investigates individual financial circumstances and advises, refers or gives grants. The education committee provides for children with clothing and (occasionally) school fees, and the council helps with holiday maintenance.

Relate
Herbert Gray College, Little Church Street, Rugby, Warks CV21 3AP
Helpline: 9 a.m.–5 p.m. weekdays 01788 573241
Web: www.relate.org.uk
Email: enquiries@relate.org.uk

Relate offers counselling and sexual function therapy all over the United Kingdom. This includes counselling for couples that are separating and divorcing.

The Samaritans
24 hour number: 08457 909090
Web: www.samaritans.org.uk

The Samaritans are famous for their telephone helpline offering (sometimes literally) a lifeline to the depressed.

UK College of Family Mediation
Alexander House, Telephone Avenue, Bristol BS1 4BS
Tel: 0117 904 7223
Fax: 0117 904 3331
Web: www.ukcfm.co.uk
E-mail: ukcfm@btclick.com

Offers a list of all groups and individuals offering family mediation in the United Kingdom.

Women's Aid Federation
PO Box 391, Bristol BS99 7WS
Helpline: 9 a.m.–9 p.m. daily 08457 023468

Information and sources of help for battered wives, including addresses of local women's refuges.

PUBLICATIONS

The Comprehensive Advice Guide to Lone Parents' Rights. June 2004 is available from www.amazon.co.uk or from One Parent Families (Freephone 0800 018 5026).

The Lone Parent Handbook 2004/05 is a comprehensive advice guide that covers the crucial issues affecting Britain's 1.75 million lone parents. It includes:

- practical advice on relationship breakdown
- domestic violence: contact and parental responsibility
- housing

- maintenance and the Child Support Agency
- benefits and tax credits
- personal finance and debt
- education and employment rights
- government schemes on training and employment
- childcare
- children's status and rights
- education for children – including bullying and truancy
- looking after children with difficult behaviour.

SUMMARY

- Don't be afraid to seek specialist advice. Information really can mean power.
- Don't be afraid to seek mediation or counselling. Each offers the chance of improving separation and divorce arrangements.

APPENDIX 2 LEGAL PROCEEDINGS

Divorce proceedings have been radically improved within the last decade. The Children Act of 1989 removed the concepts of care and control and custody, simplifying matters so that all custody of children is *joint custody*. This means that divorcing couples are now free to decide between them what provision they want to make for childcare and who will do what. Although all agreements have to satisfy the matrimonial judge, it is only if you are *un*able to reach an agreement over the children that the court will become involved.

When divorce is relatively easy

The judge needs to know that you have agreed:

- with which parent the children will live
- how often the other parent will see the children.

Provided that you are able to make such arrangements jointly, there will be no legal difficulties.

When divorce gets difficult

It is only if you are unable to make such decisions that you will need to consult a solicitor and make one or more of the following applications to the court.

- A **residence order** – this decides with whom the children will live.
- A **contact order** – this decides how often the children will see the absent parent.
- A **prohibited steps order** – this decides whether one or both parents are prohibited from behaving in a certain way, doing something or taking the children away (e.g. to the other end of the country or even to the other side of the world).
- A **specific issue order** – this is exactly what it sounds like: it decides, for example, which school a child might attend.

Divorce Aid

Web: www.divorceaid.co.uk

This is a useful web site set up by an independent group of professionals. It offers divorce advice, support and information. The welfare of the child is considered paramount and the web site promotes mediation and counselling as well as a variety of professional advice. It offers financial advice, nationwide contact with solicitors, helplines, and a teenage web site.

Advice about lawyers

It is wise to use a lawyer specialising in divorce and/or family custody issues. You need someone with expert knowledge and the solicitor who did the conveyancing for your family home probably won't possess this.

Be aware that legal costs are high, so always discuss these before taking action. You may be eligible for **legal aid**, but this is not as easy to arrange as it once was since the criteria for legal aid have been altered. It pays to be able to work out your arrangements between the two of you.

The **Legal Aid Office** is at 85 Gray's Inn Road, London WC1X 8TX. Tel: 020 7759 1140. Web: www.legal-aid.gov.uk

Conciliation

If you are in dispute, one of the first things you are legally compelled to do is to go to conciliation. The purpose of this is to discuss the issues of dispute, with the children's best interests as priority. Your children may also be asked to take part in this so that the court can understand their wishes too.

Perhaps you feel you would benefit from such proceedings even though you are not in serious dispute regarding the children. Be aware that there are **mediation** services available for precisely this purpose in most parts of the United Kingdom. Anyone can attend.

Safeguards

If you feel that there is even a hint of a custody dispute, be aware that there are certain standards that will affect a judge's ultimate decision.

1. The state of your home. Believe it or not, cleanliness is taken into account. So is the size of the home and the accommodation for the children. This is *not* to say that the children are automatically awarded to the parent with the most luxurious home – they are not. But the judge needs to feel satisfied that the surroundings are adequate. This may also include considerations such as whether there is unsuitable 'literature' left lying around. In the past, custody cases have been lost because radical political literature is on view and there are radical feminist posters on the walls. Even nude scenes by respected artists have proved risky in the past. So too are sex magazines. We are living in relatively open times, but there is no point in taking unnecessary risks with your children's future.

2. Who the children are presently living with. You stand the best chance of keeping your children if they are already living with you. The moral of this is to begin the separation as you mean to go on. Be aware that if you leave the children with the other parent for a temporary period it may be difficult to get them back.

3. Evidence that you are a good parent. Keep a diary in which you note down everything that has happened in the past and keep track of what is happening at present. You should include in it your children's statements about who they want to live with and the context in which they were made, their attitude towards your lover (if you have one) and your activities with the children. Everything should be recorded with dates. If you are in correspondence with your solicitor, include as much of this information as possible in your letters to him/her.

4. Stability is all-important. If you are living with someone, don't do any swapping about.

5. Religion can become a focus for dispute, as in a case where a mother had converted to Judaism and the father objected to the fact that their child (a Christian) might become affected by her Jewish ideas. He ended up with the child. You would be wise to play down any potential religious controversy.

6. Assessors. If it becomes necessary to get an assessment from a psychiatrist or social worker, you would be wise to try and do so through an organisation like One Parent Families (see Appendix 1). Their contacts pride themselves on giving *unbiased reports*.

7. Appearance. At the court case itself, do *not* dress scruffily. It is imperative that you look clean, neat and conservative.

It should not be necessary for the children to attend court during such disputes. Any time you may actually resolve the issue you can halt dispute proceedings.

You can also take reassurance from the fact that custody, access and maintenance can be reopened and reviewed regularly.

If you are unable to satisfactorily resolve the issue of child maintenance, you can seek the assistance of the **Child Support Agency**. Web: www.csa.gov.uk. National Helpline: PO Box 55, Brierly Hill, West Midlands DY5 1YL. Tel: Mon.–Fri. 8 a.m.–8 p.m., Saturday 9 a.m.–5 p.m. 08457 133133.

Rights of unmarried mothers

Unmarried mothers have the same rights over their children as do married parents.

Rights of unmarried fathers

Unmarried fathers only have the same rights as the unmarried mother if their name is registered on the birth certificate and if their children were born after 1 December 2004.

Unmarried fathers who do not match these criteria can gain equal rights by:

- marrying the children's mother
- re-registering the birth and adding their details to the certificate
- a written agreement with the children's mother. Forms for this purpose are available from your local County Court
- court order if agreement cannot be jointly reached.

Unfortunately many unmarried fathers wrongly assume they have the same parental rights as the mother and only discover this on separation. Separation of course is not the optimum time in which to gain them.

There are two organisations (see Appendix 1 for details) from which advice on fathers' rights can be gained. **Families Need Fathers** is a group of divorced men and women who fight for the rights of fathers when custody has been granted to the mother. **Fathers Direct** exists to support the welfare of children by the positive and active involvement of fathers and male carers in their lives.

Rights of grandparents

The bad news is that there is no such thing as a specific set of 'grandparents' rights'. Happily, though, the *child* does have the right to see not only its parents, but also those people who have played a significant role in his/her life, such as grandparents.

It is possible for matters to be resolved without going to court. There are conciliation services (see local Yellow Pages), plus grandparents can attend mediation with the parents.

Details of conciliation services and mediation services in your area are available from your solicitor, local court or local Citizen's Advice Bureau.

Some facts and figures

- The UK has 13 million grandparents.
- One in every three people over the age of fifty is a grandparent.
- The value of childcare by UK grandparents has been calculated at over £1 billion a year (children under twelve, at a cost of £2.97 per hour).
- One in five children under sixteen years old is looked after in the daytime by grandparents.
- More than one-third of grandparents spend the equivalent of three days a week caring for their grandchildren.
- In the past two generations, the number of children cared for by grandparents has jumped from 33 per cent to 82 per cent.

.../continued

> - Only one person in ten in the UK agrees that 'Grandparents have little to teach grandchildren'.
> - Three-quarters of UK adults believe that 'With so many working mothers, families need grandparents to help more and more'.

Grandparents Action Group UK
Helpline: 01952 582 621

The Grandparents Association
Moot House, The Stow, Harlow, CM20 3AG
Office/Fax: 01279 428040
Advice line: 01279 444964 (10.30 a.m.–3.30 p.m. daily with some evening sessions)
Benefits line: 01279 412963 (for members whose grandchildren are resident with them)
Web: www.grandparents-association.org.uk
Email: info@grandparents-association.org.uk

Grandparents Apart Self Help Group (GASH)
Tel: 0141 882 5658
Web: www.grandparentsapart.co.uk

CONCLUSION

The best method of dealing with separation and divorce where children are concerned is to work out the practicalities of childcare between you, and when feasible, to put the needs of the children first. Litigation is expensive, acrimonious and prolongs the children's agony. Try to manage without it if you possibly can.

APPENDIX 3 WHERE TO GET HELP WITH CHILDCARE

DAY CARE FOR CHILDREN UNDER FIVE

A relative may be able to look after your baby, or perhaps you can afford to hire outside help. Otherwise the choice lies between council or private day nurseries, and crèches provided by employers. Playgroups and nursery classes may be helpful if you have a part-time job.

Day nurseries run by local authorities

These nurseries are staffed by trained nursery and medical nurses. They are often very over-subscribed, so get your children on the waiting list immediately. Most councils give priority to single parents. If you are waiting for a nursery place *before* you find employment, you must find a job within two weeks or so of your child starting at the nursery. Most councils insist that you live or work within the local authority area and some insist that you are working for thirty hours a week, although others accept part-timers. Not all accept student parents. Cost usually depends on your income. Some councils impose a minimum charge. It is an advantage if your GP or social worker supports your application. Health visitors can also help with obtaining day nursery vacancies.

Private day nurseries
A list of these is available from your local authority's social services department, whose number will be in the telephone directory. Private day nurseries are run on similar lines to council nurseries, except that they cost more and sometimes have shorter hours.

Child-minders
A child-minder is usually a housewife with children of her own who wants a job to fit in with her domestic arrangements. She will look after your child in her own home. You should ensure that she is registered with the local authority.

It is difficult to tell how good a particular child-minder is. But you can make some attempt to find out. Call on her beforehand. Have a good look at her home, and watch the other children in the household for a while. Do they look happy or are they lying in cots with nothing to do? Find out what her programme is for the children each day. If you have any reason to think the children are not being looked after properly, get in touch with the social services department.

A child-minder's hours can usually be arranged to correspond with your working day. If you do not know any minders, the social services department keeps a list of those registered with them. Sometimes, child-minders advertise in the local newspapers or on local noticeboards.

Employers' creches
A few enlightened employers – hospitals, some unions and certain industrial companies – provide crèches for employees' children. Sometimes universities and colleges of higher education do too.

These crèches are generally supervised by trained staff and offer facilities similar to day nurseries. The advantages of having a crèche at work are tremendous. You can see your child during the day if you need to, and there is no problem about rushing from work at the end of the day.

Factory and company crèches are not registered but the personnel manager of any particular company or the local employment exchange will be able to inform you if or where they exist.

The Royal College of Nursing, 20 Cavendish Street, London W1G 0RN (tel: 020 7409 3333, 24-hour advice line 0845 772 6100, web: www.rcn.org.uk) will have information about hospital crèches. Or you can phone the secretary of your area health authority for information. A list of college crèches can be provided by the **National Union of Students**, Nelson Mandela House, 461 Holloway Road, London N7 6LJ (tel: 020 7272 8900, fax: 020 7263 57133, email: nusuk@nus.org.uk) on receipt of a large prepaid envelope.

Private (paid) help

Nannies are generally very experienced trained children's nurses who live in. You can find a nanny through a domestic employment agency (addresses of these agencies appear in the classified sections of magazines such as *The Lady*). You can place an ad looking for a nanny in these magazines. Local papers are good places to advertise, too. Some training colleges for nursery nurses like their students to obtain practical experience. So, if you apply directly to the colleges, you may be able to find a competent nanny for a less expensive wage.

Mother's helps are generally young, untrained women who normally live in, although many live out nowadays. They will hopefully be caring and sympathetic towards children, and reliable. They will usually be employed on a part-time rather than a full-time basis, since someone very young will probably find the strain of caring for children too much to take on for eight hours a day. Mother's helps can also be found through the classified columns of *The Lady*, *Nursery World* and local papers. School leavers may be interested in a job of this kind. If you contact the careers officer at your local secondary school towards the end of a term (the summer term is of course the time you are most likely to find a school leaver), he or she may be able to suggest suitable candidates.

Au pairs. You can arrange to employ an au pair through domestic employment agencies, or advertise for one in *The Times* or the *International Herald Tribune*. Although au pairs are a cheaper form of home help, they tend only to be satisfactory if you have a minor part-time job. The hazards are that their English may be non-existent and their hours will be relatively short. They live in.

Playgroups

These are part-time and are therefore only of use to part-time workers. A list of local groups will be available from the social services department or from the Citizens' Advice Bureau.

Nursery schools and nursery classes

The purpose of nursery school or class is education through play rather than childcare. Hours vary from school to school. Some operate all day; others are for mornings or afternoons only. They cater for children aged between two and five. Nursery classes are often attached to state primary schools. A list of schools and classes is available from the local education authority. It is best to apply as early as possible because there may be a waiting list, but priority is given to single parents. State nursery education is free, while private schools charge varying fees. Montessori schools are of an especially high standard.

Gingerbread

Gingerbread's local groups (see Appendix 1) run many individual schemes, such as holiday childcare and after-school care for children of all ages. The Gingerbread Holiday Scheme enables single parents to have holidays by exchanging or sharing their homes with others. Babysitting is available at the Liverpool 'pop-in' centre, where childcare arrangements for holidays are also provided.

AFTER-SCHOOL AND HOLIDAY CARE FOR SCHOOL-AGE CHILDREN

Schools

A few primary and secondary schools remain open outside school hours, running after-school provision for children of working parents. They may also run holiday play schemes. You can find out which schools do this by getting in touch with the local education authority (phone number in telephone directory).

Local authorities also run various holiday schemes and there may be others run by voluntary organisations in your area, e.g. Gingerbread (see Appendix 1). The local authority or the local library will usually have details of what is available.

Housing associations

A few housing associations also have special childcare facilities. Examples of such associations are Nina West Homes and New Swift, but for a full list get in touch with the **Housing**

Corporation, Maple House, 149 Tottenham Court Road, London W1T 7BN. Tel: 0845 230 7000. Fax: 020-7393-2111. Email: enquiries@housingcorp.gsx.gov.uk

Private help

You could advertise for help on a part-time or full-time basis to fit in with school hours and your job or commitments. A young housewife with a child of her own might fill the bill very well.

SUMMARY

- Get as much help as you can.
- Don't be afraid to approach friends, organisations.
- Use the system – single parents get priority.

APPENDIX 4 JOBS

TO WORK OR NOT TO WORK

It is important to weigh up the value of the job and the cost of childcare while you are out at work. You might be financially better off on Income Support. This has the added advantage that you will be able to look after your children personally, which, if they are very young, is of great value. Advice about benefits may be obtained from your social security office (see the telephone directory). Working people can claim benefits through their local Jobcentre Plus.

It's worth remembering, however, that there are social advantages to going to work. If you are a lone parent, you might be glad to get out of the house and mix with adults even if only for a few hours; and it also gives you a greater opportunity to meet new people.

EMPLOYMENT OPTIONS

Full-time work
The nearer your place of work is to your children's nursery or school, the better. You will need a fallback arrangement, however,

in case the children are ill, so you should know in advance who might be prepared to come in and look after them on a temporary basis. One of the best places to work (from the point of view of childcare) is at a school, as a teacher or a secretary, or on the domestic staff, since you may be able to have time off during school holidays.

If you had a career before having children, or indeed if you are still continuing with it, you of course stand the best chance of earning well by pursuing your original training or experience. It is important to emphasise that if you can continue with work which is familiar, it will make life easier. When you are coping with the trauma of separation or divorce and the strain of being a single parent *and* breadwinner, it makes sense to do what comes naturally. It also means that you are more likely to get promotion, thereby earning more. And of course, while it may well be best to stick with a job you know while the demands of separation are taking up so much of your energies, you can always look for something different once things are more settled.

If you are looking for a new job, it is certainly worth trying to find one where provision for childcare is made.

Part-time work

One way to combine part-time work with looking after the children is to take temporary jobs. If you are a secretary you can work as a 'temp', which means you are the one who decides what hours to accept. This enables you to work to fit in with your children's schedule in both term time and school holidays. You may be able to claim Income Support during the holidays when you are out of work (check with your local benefits office). There are also a number of seasonal jobs, such as work on farms and holiday (tourist) jobs. Many small businesses need part-time workers too. Enrolling at the various office and secretarial agencies in your area would be the best way to find temping jobs. Kellys and Adecco are two of the better-known agencies.

Freelance work

This is the ideal work to combine with bringing up children. Jobs such as journalism or market research, outwork or illustrating are just a few obvious ones that spring to mind. But if you don't have particular training or a special talent, you could make use of your domestic abilities to care for someone else's children, do hairdressing for friends, become a cook supplying home-made food to stores or to other mothers. One disadvantage is that your income will not be steady; another is that you will need to organise your own tax and national insurance, or pay an accountant to do so.

Residential work

A live-in job means you combine work, home and salary. It may seem the solution to many problems but one of the snags of living on top of the job is that it tends to take over your life. Most of the living-in jobs where your children will be accepted will be of a domestic variety. You might place an ad in *The Lady* or *Nursery World*, or reply to some of the advertisements you find there. Local papers also advertise positions of this kind.

Careers advice

The latest edition of the highly successful and long-established *Penguin Careers Guide* (editor Jan Widmer) is an indispensable resource for anyone seeking careers information. It contains invaluable advice on education, training and employment issues, including new information about work/life balance initiatives. More than 300 careers are covered, and for each entry there are details about the qualifications required, the nature of the work, desirable personal attributes and training, as well as advice for late starters and those returning to work, and directions on where to go for further information. This is the most authoritative and practical careers guide available.

Women's Rights at Work: A Handbook of Employment Law, by Alison Clarke (Pluto Press) outlines everything women may need to know about their legal position as regards their jobs.

SUMMARY

- Stay with your existing job if possible.
- Check the financial wisdom of work versus staying at home with the children.
- Leave no stone unturned in seeking work that (at least partially) blends with childcare.

APPENDIX 5 HOUSING

Detailed information on husbands' and wives' rights to the family home in the event of divorce is provided in *The Comprehensive Advice Guide to Lone Parents' Rights. June 2004* (see Appendix 1).

The Lone Parent Handbook 2004/05 (see Appendix 1) covers all housing matters, including:

- what to do in the event of the family property being in the husband's name, in the wife's name, or in joint names
- how to safeguard a matrimonial right
- how to claim a share of the family property during marriage
- what share you may be entitled to
- what legal arrangements are likely to be made to divide the property
- what can be done legally if you have nowhere to live after divorce
- what happens to rented property after divorce, whether it is private or council owned
- what happens if you have a joint tenancy, if the tenancy is in the husband's name or in the wife's.

MORTGAGE REPAYMENTS

If a partner suddenly has to cope with mortgage repayments single-handed, and also has to claim benefits, social security will pay the interest on the mortgage, though not the capital repayments. If you get into arrears with mortgage repayments, you will have to contact the lending source (building society or local authority) and explain the situation. Most are sympathetic and will make arrangements for you to defer capital repayments (take a 'mortgage holiday') until you have reorganised your finances and maintenance. In some cases you be able to arrange a mortgage repayment break for as long as a year. What you will effectively do is extend the period of your loan – the arrears will be added on at the end of your repayment.

If your financial situation is such that you are not able to resume mortgage payments, however, you will be forced to sell your house and give a lump sum to the building society to cover the remainder of the loan.

One way of coping with the extra sums needed to keep up your mortgage may be to take in a lodger. But check your position regarding tax before taking this step. You would also be wise to choose carefully, checking out their credentials and taking up references. Ideally, a lodger would be someone you already know, or who is known to the family.

You may find that, if your spouse has the right to a lump sum from the proceeds of selling the house, the remaining money is not enough to put down on a cheaper property. In these circumstances, avoid selling the house if you possibly can. The Child Poverty Action Group (see Appendix 1) may be able to offer you advice on coping with the mortgage.

FINDING A NEW HOME

If you can afford to do so, it is sensible to buy a house. If you cannot afford to buy, however, there are alternatives. The first is to rent a home.

Private Renting

The best way to find a flat or house is to consult estate agents, read the small ads in local newspapers, ask your friends.

Council Renting

You can find out how easy or difficult this may be by visiting the housing department of the local council (address in the phone book). Some areas, such as big cities, have long waiting lists for council accommodation, while others have empty houses waiting for occupation.

Councils will normally only house families and old people. A single parent with children counts as a family. A pregnant woman doesn't, although the rules change if she is homeless. Even if the council has nothing for you immediately, it is worth putting your name down on their waiting list. And you have to ensure that your name remains on a council list by reapplying at whatever intervals the local authority specifies.

If you are actually homeless (with children), the council has a duty to house you. The difficulty here is that you may find yourself placed in substandard accommodation, or lodged for months in a seedy private hotel.

Although, in theory, the council should eventually rehouse you in reasonable accommodation, this is sometimes not possible because of housing shortages. If, because of housing difficulties, there is any likelihood that your children might actually be taken away from you, get in touch with Shelter or the Catholic Housing

Aid Society (see below for addresses). One Parent Families (see Appendix 1) is used to fighting these battles too, so you can ask them for help.

Housing Associations

These provide a third form of housing. Here you invest a small premium in state-subsidised property and/or pay a reasonable rent (again state subsidised). In return, you become a member of one of a variety of housing associations. In some you gain a capital investment in the property as you continue to pay, and when you want to leave you will be able to get out of it at least what you put in. In others, you have the advantage of living in good accommodation at an extremely low rent. In yet others, you become part of a co-ownership scheme. This means that everyone in your group or block jointly owns the whole collection of properties and is not only responsible for individual accommodation but also for the administration of the properties as a whole. This last group of associations works on several levels, depending on the particular scheme, from families in individual apartments to groups of people living communally. It may shortly be possible to purchase your accommodation after living in it for some years.

One Parent Families (see Appendix 1) will be able to advise on local schemes, while general advice can be sought from the **National Housing Federation**, Lion Court, Procter Street, London WC1V 6NY. Tel: 020-7067-1010. Email: info@housing.org.uk. Some of the housing associations throughout the country are specially geared to single parents, or give priority to them, and some incorporate special childcare projects.

As with most types of housing, there are usually waiting lists. But this type of accommodation tends to become available faster than others and it is worthwhile registering as soon as you think there is a possibility that you may need somewhere to live.

Licensed Squatting

As a last resort – and I emphasise this because squatting usually involves hard work and privation – licensed squatting might provide you with short-life accommodation. The advantage of licensed squatting is that, if you have a family, this may advance you in the queue for local authority housing. Licensed squatting entails paying a minimal rent for the use of property that is due for demolition in a short time but is just about habitable. Many local councils let out this property on short leases and it is official, legal and legitimate. It is not to be confused with illegal squatting where homeless people break into empty property and start living there. Shelter (see below for details) will advise on the feasibility of licensed squatting in individual cases.

HOUSING AID

Shelter
88 Old Street, London EC1V 9HU
Free helpline: 0808 800 4444
Web:www.shelter.org.uk
Email: info@shelter.org.uk

A national campaign for the homeless, Shelter has aid offices in England, Scotland and Wales and will supply a list of these on request. It exists to help people with all kinds of housing problems, including those arising from family break-up. Once clients have come to them with a specific housing problem, they are taken on *until the problem has been solved*.

Catholic Housing Aid Society
Advice line: 020 7723 5928 Monday, Tuesday and Wednesday from 10 a.m.–1 p.m., 2 p.m.–5 p.m., Thursday 10 a.m.–1 p.m.

CHAS works in a similar way to Shelter. It has housing offices around the country and offers independent advice regarding housing and debt. It is a member of the Housing Law Practitioners Association and is open to people of all faiths.

Both Gingerbread and One Parent Families (see Appendix 1 for details) can help with housing registers and housing advice.

Advice for squatters

LandlordZone provides an excellent page setting out the rights of landlords and squatters regarding squatted accommodation. Go to: www.landlordzone.co.uk/squatters.htm

SUMMARY

- If you can possibly stay on in your present family home, this is the best thing to do because it is familiar to your children, will be reassuring to you all and will be one less change to cope with.
- If this is impossible, you must seek expert legal advice over your legal rights to maintenance and provision for housing. For property advice and information on rights, contact one of the housing aid organisations (see above).

ACKNOWLEDGEMENTS

Many thanks to the people who helped me with their advice and encouragement, both now and thirty years ago when an earlier version of this book was written. Many good wishes to Elizabeth Muirhead for legal advice, Phillip Hodson for a mature overview, the Adlerian Society for fostering Alfred Adler's remarkable and intelligent methods of child-rearing, Steve Gove for his meticulous editing and Victoria Hooper-Duckham for her illustrations. Thanks too to managing editor Jane Donovan, designer Richard Mason and publisher and old friend Jeremy Robson.